# ONE WEEK LOAN

A

**RHP**

**Russell House Publishing**

First published in 2005 by:
Russell House Publishing Ltd.
4 St. George's House
Uplyme Road
Lyme Regis
Dorset DT7 3LS

Tel: 01297-443948
Fax: 01297-442722
e-mail: help@russellhouse.co.uk
www.russellhouse.co.uk

British Library Cataloguing-in-publication Data:

A catalogue record for this book is available from the British Library.

ISBN: 1-903855-53-5

Typeset by TW Typesetting, Plymouth, Devon
Printed by Antony Rowe, Chippenham

### About Russell House Publishing

RHP is a group of social work, probation, education and youth and community work practitioners and academics working in collaboration with a professional publishing team.
Our aim is to work closely with the field to produce innovative and valuable materials to help managers, trainers, practitioners and students.
We are keen to receive feedback on publications and new ideas for future projects.
For details of our other publications please visit our website or ask us for a catalogue. Contact details are on this page.

# Contents

Dedicated to Rosemary Lillian Harris:
for love, fortitude and courage.

# Acknowledgements

No person or idea exists in a void. As a writer and as a collection of ideas presented here, much is owed to those who have supported me over the years. Special thanks must go to Jessica Gwyther, for always knowing what is important. I am forever in debt to my surrogate self-belief systems, Justin and Claire Hoggans and Martin and Jane Shotbolt for their unflinching faith. Jo Bush and Jools Hesketh for sponsoring my itinerant lifestyle. To Jason Trevitt, Steve Sawyer, Merrick Williams, Claire Miller and Simon Roberts for making me laugh when I was down, and bringing me down when I was having a laugh. To Amanda and Ruby Wilsdon for being so magnificent. To all the writers cited in the book, but especially Stanton Peele and Richard DeGrandpre in particular, whose writing, insight and personal support has been invaluable. Special thanks must also go to those editors who originally published my work. Addiction journals are not known for courageous publishing, the exceptions are Deirdre Boyd of *Addiction Today* and Denise Winn of the Human Givens: *Radical Psychology Today*. It has been great to work with them and I hope that my amendments to these articles do not do too much violence to their sensitive and clear editorial styles. Special thanks must also go to my editor, John Pitts, for teasing this book out of me and whose assuredness has been the perfect antidote to my 'first book anxiety syndrome'. And last but not least to Geoffrey Mann, the managing director of Russell House Publishing. Relationships are never supposed to be easy in the shotgun weddings of writers and publishers. But his enthusiasm, openness and friendship were immensely important in the development of this book and the titles to follow.

# Foreword

Deirdre Boyd*

The one indisputable fact about addiction – or dependency, as the scientists prefer to call it – is that there is no one cause creating it and no one solution to recover from its thrall. Addiction is a kaleidoscopic pattern of all that is human nature: facets of our biological, psychological and social selves interact to offer myriad patterns. Insights into addiction give us insights into humankind in all its fascinating complexity, the differences often existing only by 'degree' or intensity.

Phil Harris knows this and eschews in this book the simplistic explanations of addiction espoused for convenience by too many workers in the field who should know better.

Wisdom comes from the long marriage of knowledge and experience. Academics and clinicians need to know more about each other's work, and how they can be mutually beneficial, before they can offer wise and compassionate solutions to both sufferers from addiction (with their families) and the policy-makers who wield the power to help or hinder care.

Academics, sadly, tend to devalue colleagues who gain experience, saying that they lose impartiality rather than recognising the birth of wisdom. In this environment, it is not surprising that Phil Harris can feel that he is regarded not merely as a rebel but as a heretic. Yet his words contain eminent common sense.

Addicts are not laboratory animals, and laboratories are not the real world. Some knowledge can be gained there, particularly into how our natural chemicals in our brains affect and are affected by artificial chemicals such as alcohol, legal and illegal drugs and tobacco – and by brain chemicals generated by 'addictive behaviours' such as starving, bingeing, exercising, having sex, overworking, gambling, and the like. But laboratory work is not the whole solution; even if it were, it is only in its infancy. For example, laboratory work on artificial 'feel-good' chemicals (SSRIs or selective serotonin re-uptake inhibitors, to replace natural serotonin) did not take into account how its users would act in the outside world, nor did they account for all the 'receptors' or facets of serotonin – with the result that depressed people who used SSRIs then used alcohol or used other drugs became even more suicidal. There is no magic silver bullet.

Addicts are people, usually people who need guidance not merely to recover from their addictive behaviour but also from damaged childhoods. This is the truly human

---

*Deirdre Boyd is CEO of the Addiction Recovery Foundation, editor of *Addiction Today* magazine and cofounder of the Unity group and the UK/European Symposium on Addictive Disorders.

face of addiction. As children, they were never taught to problem-solve life. They were given no lessons in holding the emotions of living. If mood-altering substances could change a child's mood, and they are taught no alternatives, then that is a natural course to take. For many, recovery from addiction is also a cognitive recovery from childhood.

We can choose to take hold of our lives only when wise people give us the facts on which we can safely base decisions. Then and only then do we have choices. Readers should thank Phil Harris for opening up these choices with this wise book.

# Introduction: Biology or Belief?

*It is an important feature of the ideological system to impose on people the feeling that they really are incompetent to deal with these complex and important issues: they had better leave it to the captain. One device is to develop a star system, an array of figures who are often media creations or creations of the academic propaganda establishment, whose deep insights we are supposed to admire and to whom we must happily and confidently assign the right to control our lives . . .*

Naom Chomsky

The one thing that distorts reality more than drugs themselves is the fear that people are taking them. I was once interviewed about young people's drug use by a journalist from a mass circulation international magazine. She asked me what I thought, in this regard, was the biggest threat to young people today. I told her I thought it was the media. Through sensationalist journalism, newspaper horror stories, celebrity drug prevention campaigns and ratings-driven soap operas, drugs have become an everyday cultural experience. Whilst drugs' effects remain extraordinary, in the true sense of the word, they are as familiar to us today as branded labels and chocolate bars. The inhibiting 'fear of the unknown' factor has been replaced by the encouraging 'every one my age is doing it factor' (South, 1999). Inflation of the figures makes it seem a cultural norm that young people are now enmeshed in the drug culture, in the process lowering its unacceptability.

Thumbing through my complimentary copy of the magazine when the article was published, I found no mention of my contribution. Instead there were lurid descriptions of a 14 year-old's agonising withdrawal after three weeks of heroin use, who demanded her mother 'cut off her legs' the pain was so bad, and a doctor's despairing claim of overwhelming numbers of 11–13 year-olds coming in for in-patient detoxification. In my many years as a drug worker I never encountered this. So I phoned the hospital concerned but they refused to give me the figures. My thinking about the media's role was, sadly, confirmed yet again.

It seems that what is most important to the media, is to portray as vividly as possible the dangers of drug use as a degenerative condition leading inexorably to the destruction of the user. This is done in the hope of deterring people from experimenting. The fact that drug use has continued to climb exponentially has not discouraged anyone from this strategy. And the detrimental effect of this media coverage is never considered at all. The collection of articles and presentations within this book are an attempt to redress this balance. They stem from personal and professional experience as a drugs worker where I was continually confronted by a discrepancy between what I read about addiction and what I actually worked with on a day to day basis. This divergence led me to question much of what was accepted in practice and opened new ways of understanding the problem and its treatment. These considerations were presented in a collection of articles and conference speeches written over a three year period. In order to rationalise the reading, changes and alterations have been made to cohere this broad range of issues into one book. But the central focus of re-evaluating the folk wisdom, popular science and sensationalism that have come to cement public opinion and dominate professional practice in addiction and treatment remains.

This is because such well intentioned misinformation has obstructed the under-standing of the real nature of addiction. The current experience of addiction is a very new phenomenon. Historically man has made use of drugs since the Palaeolithic period. Richard Morris, director of the British Council for Archaeology, has even suggested renaming it 'the Stoned Age' because of increasingly common references to cannabis, opium and other drugs in excavation reports. Yet we only begin to find references to the kind of mass addictive behaviour that we witness today as late as the 1700s. It was then that both the theological and medical authorities in America and Western Europe started to take an interest in drug use and began to push for greater social control of freely available narcotics. This movement was to set out the parameters of our concerns regarding the 'disease' of addiction, and all current legal frameworks and treatment philosophies claim direct lineage to this period. The first chapter in this book, *A Very Brief History of Addiction Treatment*, charts how these assumptions have shaped our thinking and cemented a potent popular vision of addiction and drug use; but one which has never been validated.

Swathes of evidence undermine the accepted wisdom of addiction as a biological compulsion. A close look at these deterministic assumptions exposes their limitations and raises important questions about the future development of treatment. The notion that drugs possess a 'must have' power which induces compulsivity in humans is the cornerstone of current biomedical thinking and one apparently born out in extensive animal experimentation. Early experiments conducted on mammals in the 1950s demonstrated that lab animals would self-administer narcotics or electrical stimulation directly into their own brains through electrodes, even to the point of death if given the opportunity (Glynn, 1999). The central drive was believed to be pleasure seeking. It is questionable whether the findings can be applied to humans. The initial response in humans to drugs such as heroin is physical repulsion, whilst other drugs such as cannabis need to be used repeatedly before the mood altering effects are learned. However, as animal research directly serves to inform social policy on drug control and augment current visions of addiction as 'loss of control' it is critical to explore this research more deeply. Chapter 2, *Of Mice and Men*, scrutinises this area of study to identify what this research really tells us about the nature of addiction. This will also provide the opportunity to identify the principle biological concepts in addiction and illuminate their elasticity. Some of these key research findings are then applied to the human experience in Chapter 3. *The Myth of Overdose* explores how pertinent it is to question some of these concepts if we wish to reduce the unnecessary and tragic loss of human life related to drug consumption.

We cannot rely on the much maligned rat for conclusive answers relating to humans. When we take a look across different historical periods and cultural groups we witness a very different experience of drugs and addiction. In India, where heroin has been used for centuries, we did not see the same addictive behaviour as in the West until recently. One North Indian drug user I treated had never experienced withdrawal symptoms while he was living in India but did experience it once he had moved to the UK. Other clients have reported withdrawal symptoms from heroin when visiting certain places. And tellingly, many symptoms of withdrawal in the strung out user evaporated not when they used drugs but when they purchased drugs. Outside our culture we see diverse experiences of the same drug. Tribes in South America use alcohol as part of religious ceremonies and, despite being in a state of chronic inebriation, they still observe strict social taboos against incest even during orgiastic sex ceremonies. They also don't experience hangovers.

Contrary to public opinion, this variance cannot be accounted for within genetics models. Despite this, genetics, combined with neurology, now promises the answers to addiction and is much vaunted in the media. This line of research continually heralds the discovery of the genetic origin of addiction, but the results never stand up to further scrutiny. Much of the research focuses on the inheritable abnormality of neurological receptors which engage with the brain's natural chemical messengers such as dopamine. However, dopamine plays a multifaceted role in the operation of the brain and it is impossible that just one specific effect should emerge as a result of this deficiency. Research into the neurology of abnormal behaviour is continually described as promising. But, as American psychiatrist and psychotherapist Peter Breggin (1993) points out, they have been promising since 1820 and have still not delivered. Considering all the evidence, the esteemed biologist and statistician, Richard Lewontin (2000) could only conclude '. . . the notion that the war on drugs will be won by genetic engineering belongs to Cloud Cuckoo Land . . .' The scope of genetics in the field of addiction is examined in Chapter 4, *Engineering Genetics*.

There is nothing in genetic research which can account for compulsive usage or explain the cultural and situational factors which modify drug using behaviours – unless it is truly believed that soldiers have a receptor site which craves heroin only when in combat zones, or that a 30 year-old alcoholic has a gene which makes him age out of this behaviour at 55. If we wish to understand these problems we must revise some of our deep assumptions about human nature and change. Chapter 5,

*The Binds that Tie*, will reorientate our thinking about addiction and redefine it in a cultural and social context. This is to recognise the problem not as an intractable disease but as a dynamic process of interaction between an individual and their environment. Within this, research identifies that many people, if not the majority, cut down or quit drugs, smoking and alcohol without any recourses to treatment whatsoever (Vaillant, 1995; Kandel, 1995). This is rarely considered, and the underlying processes which allow individuals to do so are ignored rather than imported into improving effective treatment models. Key mechanisms in the natural remission process are highlighted in Chapter 6, *Natural Born Quitters*, which examines drug use across the life course; and its relevance for young people's treatment is detailed in Chapter 7, *The Apprenticeship for Life*.

Other research, in the alcohol field, has shown that clients' readiness to change exerts a far greater influence on successful outcomes than pharmacological support (Hernandez-Avila et al., 1999). Here psycho-cultural expectancy outperforms psycho-pharmacology. Cognition plays such a crucial role in the decision to change and treatment outcome that the process of intentional change will be considered in Chapter 8, *Well Intentioned Change*. It provides an overview of this process and includes broad findings in treatment outcome. The process of intentional change has become such an important foundation of current practice in the UK that it is expanded upon in greater depth. Chapter 9, *Counselling and Other Sacred Cows*, explores the process of working with counselling teams to amend practice. There is a need to respect counselling as more than a tool but an extension of the workers' ethics. Particular attention will focus on motivational interviewing in Chapter 10, *Ignition of Change*, and its relevance that this much vaunted intervention has had for the field as a whole.

Special consideration is given to the dual diagnosis client and the change process in Chapter 11, *Bi-Cycle of Change*. The complex cognitive process of change is made ever more sophisticated in the client with multiple needs. Mental health, personality disorder and learning disability all render the individual vulnerable to the cultural detachment we define as addiction. The complexity of these issues is further elucidated in Chapter 12, *Keep Taking the Tablets*, which considers how the latest findings in relapse prevention may support the gains of this vulnerable client group in sustaining change.

What constitutes effective treatment is continually debated within the field. The $36 million study, Project MATCH, attempted to identify which psychosocial treatment approaches were the most effective for alcoholism. However, its findings were equivocal, placing all treatment modalities as statistically equal in terms of outcomes. Outside of the modalities tested, clients who did well shared situational factors such as readiness to change, abatement of social pressures and access to positive peer groups. Prevalence, duration or intensity of alcohol consumption had no bearing on these outcomes. This is supported by clinical research showing that addicts themselves considered biological symptoms such as withdrawal the least influential reason for relapse (Marlatt and Gordon, 1985). But this has not prevented Enoch Gordis, president of the influential US pro-biomedical National Institute on Alcohol and Alcoholism (NIAAA), from declaring that research will now focus on the biological mechanisms of abnormal consumption (NIAAA Press Release, 1996). Large meta-analysis has highlighted critical issues in treatment outcomes yet MATCH failed to find significant differences. Chapter 13, *Project Match or Project Mess?* explores why these findings were inconclusive and what this suggests for the field.

In contrast to the legal framework and cultural attitudes towards illegal drugs, Chapter 14, *Better than Well*, examines the marketing, politics and consequences of Prozac. More than any other prescription drug, Prozac's success can only be considered as a powerful confluence of science, politics and capitalism. It provides an interesting counterpoint which illuminates the contradiction innate in our cultural consciousness towards drug use and its value; where, under the auspices of 'science', human nature itself is deemed subservient to the all powerful chemical interaction.

So much of current biomedical treatment fails because it endorses the very powerlessness of the individual, and administers to the self-defeating expectations which promote rather than insulate against failure. Pharmacology sells the modern myth that the world can restore the individual, when the central problem is how individuals learn to restore themselves, and overcome the forces of their world. Now, even the choice of whether or not to enter treatment is to be denied by the external forces which dominate the inner lives of so many. Drugs work has been annexed as an extension of the criminal justice system. We are no longer sure whether we are diseasing the criminal or criminalising the diseased in what has mutated into a medical justice approach to addiction. Whilst investment in support is essential, there are dangers that the current obsessions ingrained in therapeutic programmes are herding people down a dead end. Treatment programmes may be running at full speed but they may also be running down the wrong road. We run the risk of smashing our hopes and aspirations for more enlightened, effective treatment against the limits of our own thinking. We must try to replace reaction with reason, if our response is to be any more than simply drug induced.

Based on 'Addiction: Biology or Belief?' *New Therapist*, Dec 2000

# Chapter 1

# A Very Brief History of Addiction Treatment

*But I'll tell you something about drugs – I used to do drugs – but I'll tell you something honestly about drugs – honestly – and I know it's not a very popular idea, you don't hear it very often any more, but it is the truth. I had a great time doing drugs. Never murdered anybody, never robbed anyone, never raped anyone, never beat anyone, never lost a job, a car, a wife or kids . . . laughed my arse off, and went about my day. Sorry. Now, where's my commercial?'*

Bill Hicks

Sometimes it is not enough to think about drugs. Instead we must consider how we have come to think about them in the way that we do. Working with chaotic users, it soon occurred to me that everything I had been taught about the biology of addiction consistently appeared at odds with my daily experience. This made me wonder where our current thinking originated from and why were these beliefs sustained in light of so much disparity. The answer lies in the ideological assumptions that underpin our current practice. As an old Chinese proverb surmised; the last to realise the sea is the fish. Until we can see beyond the narrow, historically constructed vision of addiction, we remain limited in our ability to deal with problematic drug use.

## Archaeology of addiction

The use of intoxicants has a very long and pragmatic history. Because of contaminated water supplies, five per cent proof ales, ciders and mead were the staple drinks of the lower classes from at least the 8th century in Britain. This alcohol was regulated and taxed by the Church (Edwards, 2002). Given this backdrop of everyday consumption, it is notable that the first endemic rise in alcohol 'abuse' only occurred in the 18th century during the industrial revolution, when the demand for mass labour to fuel production drew unskilled rural populations into urban slums in huge numbers. Not only did this destroy the lifestyle of the rural classes, and the informal social controls and regulations they had evolved around ale consumption, it also occurred at a time when new alcohol technology was emerging.

The distillation of juniper berries was already established in Holland. So it was with the Dutch William of Orange's coronation and blessing that 60 per cent proof gin become widely available in Britain (Edwards, 2002). This culturally novel substance, with no evolved custom of usage, devastated the already miserable lives of impoverished masses. Living in utter deprivation and working relentless hours in dangerous factories, gin became the only release. Civil disorder, religious blasphemy, violence and mortality rates rocketed, and led, for the first time, to physicians' interest in this social sphere. From 1700–1735, the amount of gin on which tax was collected rose from half a million to five million gallons, excluding the massive illicit market estimated at 50 million gallons (Brownlee, 2002). In 1736, the Gin Law was passed, making the beverage prohibitively expensive (Warner, 1999). Riots ensued, the law was flouted and consumption soared to a staggering 14 gallons a year per male in London alone.

In America, things were little better. From the industrial societies in the east of the country to the remote pioneer stations in the west, there was appalling human suffering and unrest, causing increasing concern amongst the residual Puritan bourgeoisie. Whilst political reformists blamed shocking living conditions, religious evangelists started to blame alcohol. In 1784, Philadelphia physician Dr Benjamin Rush published his book *An Inquiry into the Effects of Spirituous Liquors on the Human Body and the Mind*. Within it he described the 'moral and physical thermometer'. Using state of the art medical 'science', his diagram of a thermometer, calibrated from 70 to minus 70, arranged drinks in a hierarchy. It started, at the top, with water, charted as the bringer of 'health and wealth' and descended through beverages by strength, culminating in Pepper in Rum, which was linked with the most dire outcomes, including palsy, apoplexy, hatred of just government, murder, suicide or death at the gallows. The thermometer created a causal link between antisocial behaviour, crime, sickness and death within a continuum of alcohol consumption, *without any reference at all to social factors*.

This kitchen sink medicine and religious condemnation was a winning recipe for the Christian bourgeoisie. Rush's book sold over 170,000 copies, and he swore to create a temperance movement to ensure 'the use of spirits [would be] as uncommon in families as a drink made from a solution of arsenic or a decoction of hemlock'. By 1835 the American Temperance Society was claiming 1.5 million members and was exporting its zealous ideology to the world via both the prohibitionists, who focused on the causal agent, alcohol, and campaigned vociferously for its abolition, and the salvationists, who were concerned with saving sufferers from the new disease of alcoholism. These assumptions about alcohol would define the 20th century's cultural stance on intoxication, with far reaching ramifications. Culture does not merely bias our opinions; it defines the legal, social and political structures that we operate in as human beings (Plotkin, 2002). These structures have real physical consequences for those under their ubiquitous duress or for those expelled from them.

## Better by law

This huge cultural shift needs to be set in context. To maintain the rise of industrialisation, a new social order was required: one based not on the flux of the seasons, as in agricultural society, but on the perpetual production lines demanded by industry. In the army, factories, hospitals and schools, there was a shift towards discipline and the standardisation of behaviour, as the French philosopher Michel Foucault (1991) has described. A new and unprecedented conformity was drilled into the masses as part of the rationalist agenda of 'betterment' that emerged with the Enlightenment. Self-regulation in sustaining one's commitment to this new conformism became the defining virtue of the new middle classes. It surfaced in the individual realm as a new civility, the social realm in legal reforms and the spiritual realm as a Calvinistic stoicism (Langford, 2002). Those that did not conform were by default unreasonable, unproductive, criminal and spiritually degenerate. Heavy alcohol consumption had been merely a bad habit. Now it was a shameful, reprehensible weakness, characterised as a 'loss of control'. Unable to operate within the demands of the new social order, they would have to live a lost life outside of them.

By 1840 new evangelical groups such as the Washingtonians were establishing themselves with the mission to save these lost souls. These souls were, however, getting hard to find. In the US, the success of temperance political campaigning meant prohibition was enacted in 13 states by 1855 (Davenport-Hines, 2001). It forced the unrepentant even further into a shadow society of illicit consumption. In the UK, crippling taxes had priced gin out of the market, whilst social reforms had improved living conditions. And the lower classes had time to learn new self-regulating customs around their gin consumption.

Moreover, in the 19th century global trade and domestic chemistry had generated a boom in more exotic intoxicants (Jay, 2000). Opium, nitrous oxide, morphine, cocaine and hashish were used on a scale not rivalled in our century. Whilst the Victorians' appetite for mysterious intoxicants outpaced we post-modernists, these foreign substances soon became subsumed into the temperance agenda (Berridge, 1999). Prohibitionists started taking an interest, for instance, in the British monopoly on opium export to China. Here they had little power other than moral condemnation in which to shame the degenerate trade (Cohen, 1999). Opium use was endemic, the prohibitionists reported, even though investigations by the British, Portuguese and Dutch found scant evidence that opium use was problematic in China, ascertaining recreational use was the norm.

This would all culminate, in the US, in complete prohibition against international trafficking in drugs and alcohol (Davenport-Hines, 2001). The new laws, enacted by 1927, criminalised drug traffickers and users throughout the member nations that signed these treaties, and these remain in place today. The US moral vanguard remains as potent today as then, to the extent that the US will still only issue grant aid to countries that subscribe to its narcotic control policies (Cohen, 1994). Whilst total prohibition on alcohol was to fail in America, with Repeal in 1933, agencies that had fought a futile war against alcohol were simply reconstituted to fight the futile war against drugs (Durlacher, 2000). The threat of drugs continues to offer leverage for the expansion of these agencies such as the Drug Enforcement Agency, domestic police forces and HM Customs and Excise, which we also trust for information gathering. Their interests are inextricably woven in the evil menace of drugs. Yet, despite over $35 billion invested by the US government alone, drugs still account for eight per cent of world trade at present. Such failure is always construed as demonstrating the need for even more resources and expansion of the very same international bureaucracies that are failing.

The trickle-down results of drug prohibition were rapid. In the US, people who had access to cheap opiates were suddenly reduced to penury as prices and restrictions increased. Most visibly affected were heavy users, who now set about eking out a living, searching for scrap junk to pay for the drug. Not only was the term 'junkie' born, but the social conditions that determined their lifestyle were created (Durlacher, 2000) as they too became ostracised from cultural institutions. Forced together by their poverty, new criminal status and social exclusion, a new underclass of poor clustered into one narrow social niche. A new cultural identity was created, with its own rituals, etiquette and permissible behaviours, for those disconnected from mainstream life. This also served to cement the self-debilitating expectations of enslavement to the drug. The pursuit of the next fix became the only meaningful activity available. Once again, it was far too easy to look at these impoverished individuals and claim their destitution was caused by drug use, rather than by the very social policies designed to save them.

## Diseased souls

By 1873, the National Temperance Society was calling for special inebriation asylums for drunkards. 'Moral therapy' had been developed to help those with deviant behaviours such as mental illness, and this was to be applied to drinkers. This view reached its height of influence in the 1930s when in America, Doctor William Silkworth, the first to develop a treatment programme for alcoholics, asserted that addiction was an innate allergy unique to certain individuals. One of his unsuccessful patients was William Wilson, who combined Silkworth's ideas with that of the Calvinist temperance movements when he helped found the Alcoholics Anonymous Fellowship in 1935. 'Bill W' drew directly from the practices and assumptions of the salvationists and from the emergent medical concept of the innate biological allergy (Levine, 1979). God and disease became fused in a programme that sold itself on the promise that adherence would ensure cure through a divine and personal revelation. It squared the perennial paradox of addiction: how to treat a disease whose defining symptom is the want of the medication.

Whilst AA remained an insular, informal self-help group, it soon drew wider support from science, most notably from psychiatrist Ernest Jellinek, based at Yale University. He propagated a new narco-pathology that was in keeping with the morally defective vision of addiction. He carried out research that appeared to support the thesis of alcoholism as a 'progressive disease' and reinforced the need for abstinence (Jellinek, 1952, 1960). However, his research subjects were AA members, already inculcated with a deeply temperate set of beliefs, which were merely elucidated in the research. But the message, not the methodology, gained popular and scientific support.

Within the realm of narcotics, the continued focus on the biological mechanism of addiction has followed in the wake of Dr Vincent Dole and Dr Marie Nyswander's (1967) influential work in the 1960s which described addiction as the outcome of neurochemical deficiency in certain individuals' brains. They proposed that those unable to manufacture natural painkillers or stimulants would have enhanced effects from these drugs. This exposure would compromise the brain's capacity to produce these neurochemicals further, demanding continued usage. This also suggested a genetic link. Such thinking led to the prescribing of the heroin substitute methadone which was envisaged as a lifelong treatment, just as insulin is for diabetics.

The concept of addiction as an innate biological problem located within an individual has gone on to find expression in neurology (see Nutt, 1996) and genetics (see Blum and Payne, 1992). We will explore the definitions and conceptual frameworks that these disciplines have propounded in detail in the following chapters. But we must recognise that neurology and genetics have yet to fulfil the promise of treatment for this innate problem of addiction. Even though, as we shall see, both the notion of an addict psychology and addiction as a progressive disease have been refuted by research (see Miller, 1996), Jellinek's ideas remain common currency throughout the treatment field and in popular thinking, through the vociferous dissemination of these ideas through the mass media (Roizen, 1998).

## Media rare

Dramatisation of the evils of drugs began in 1894, in the earliest days of cinema, with the very first 'drug' movie, *Opium Joint*. It depicted squalid Chinese opium dens which at the time were actually popular tourist traps (Stevenson, 2000). But the basic formula was to be endlessly repeated. Stereotypes of unscrupulous ethnic dealers, decent heroes turned bad and busty young heroines abandoning themselves to wanton sexual passions fuelled the popular imagination. In 1921 the Association of the Motion Picture Industry advised against any glamorisation of 'scenes which show the use of narcotics and other unnatural practices dangerous to social mortality' (Stevenson, 2000). Eventually it was forbidden to draw any attention to drugs. But a boom in (s)exploitation movies was already underway. Although these movies could not get certificates to be shown in movie theatres, travelling entrepreneurs such as Dwayne Esper, would set up marquees on the edge of town showing their low-budget extravaganzas. These films depicted a descent into debauchery and drug induced death from illicit substances which neither the filmmakers nor the audiences knew anything about. Movies like *The Derelict*, *Devil's Needle* or *The Pace That Kills* attracted huge audiences who were both shocked and titillated by these Temperance fantasies of addiction.

Restrictions on the depiction of drug use remain today. In the UK, the ITC, which licenses independent television stations, states in its code of practice that 'drug and solvent abuse should not be shown in such a way as to appear problem free or glamorous' (www.itc.org.uk). Similar restrictions apply to radio. Only problematic use can be depicted, to ward off experimentation, regardless of a broader social experience. Fears that TV portrayal of problem-free drug use might adversely affect the vulnerable were dispelled by a survey, which showed that most young people rejected the media's opportunistic moralising as feeble and distant from their own experience (Wells, 2000). Lord Holme, the British Standards Commission's chairman, still could not refrain from moralising over these research findings and missing the point entirely: 'If [the media] is to play an effective part in the fight against drug abuse, then its portrayals must be more realistic' (Wells, 2000).

Yet realism does not include portrayal of non-problematic use. It is confined to ghoulish photographs of tragic young women, such as Leah Betts, who have died in drug related incidents. Young people are more at risk of accidental death from a fairground ride than they are from Ecstasy (Williamson, 1997). One can only imagine public outcry if a photograph of a teenager mangled in a funfair tragedy was splashed across the front pages. But the narco-voyeurism of an earlier age is still culturally permissible. Not only does this make media shock tactics and information risible to young people; it renders the everyday experience of drugs wholly invisible. Such emotionality effectively prevents informed public debate.

## The watchmen

Governments have increasingly turned to science to defend moral and political positions. Research that supports its position on drugs is gleefully seized upon, regardless of its quality. As internationally respected drug expert Michael Gossop (1993) has pointed out, one poorly constructed research paper published in a respected medical journal that suggested cannabis caused brain damage was enough to justify 'the continuation and strengthening of every possible measure to suppress cannabis'.

Science has truly emerged as the new salvationist, upholding moral beliefs rather than demonstrating empirical truths. The National Institute of Drug Abuse and the European Council, which controls funding for research into addiction, will not support research into recreational drug use, nor even permit the expression 'drug use' to appear in official documents. The term has to be 'abuse' (Cohen, 1994). Research, most of which is carried out in the US, is biased towards investigations of biological compulsion and problematic use. This closes important avenues of understanding. For example, recognising how recreational users remain immunised from problematic use or how drug users mature out of use without recourse to treatment (Stall and Biernacki, 1986) could provide key information for developing more effective treatment programmes. But these are taboo areas in a disease ideology. The moral stance of 'scientific' research has done much to undermine belief in governments' candour in providing accurate information about drug use or assist those who are considering use or go on to experience problems.

## Treatment breakdown

Collectively these values have equated the drug users as the culturally 'subhuman'. Where basic rights may be taken from them and they may be subjected to 'treatment' to break through the 'denial' which supposedly insulates problematic users from their own depravity. The AA model demands a user surrender totally to the treatment's ideology, with any divergence considered 'addict talk'. This culminated, in the 1950s in a particularly aggressive form of AA in California which attracted large numbers of alcohol and drug users. In a small club house rented for regular meetings, the 'encounter group', as it termed itself cultivated its own brand of confrontation. Those present would choose a member of the group and break them down psychologically through powerful and personal criticism. This, it was claimed, had to be done to rebuild the 'defective' personality (Kennard, 1998). Led by the charismatic Chuck Dederich, the group broke away from AA and soon dubbed itself the Concept movement, initiating the first modern residential treatment programmes. Besides encounter sessions, hard labour and public humiliation were prescribed. Addicts had their heads shaved, and were forced to wear nappies or signs around their necks with shaming slogans. In 1973, Concept declared itself a religion and soon acquired cult-like status. Dederich was busy demanding sterilisation of his followers, when he was arrested for attempted murder. He had placed a rattlesnake in the mail box of a lawyer who was trying to spring a member from his community.

In their review of treatment for heroin users, drug experts Tom Carnwath and Ian Smith (2002) describe the emergence of 'rough' treatment centres in other parts of the world. In Yekaterburg, Russia, dealers are beaten up and users are chained to radiators in keeping with the concept that 'a drug addict is a wild beast, an animal, who cannot be treated with pity'. Elsewhere in Russia, only recently has a new form of brain lobotomy for drug users been banned (Paton-Walsh, 2002).

In Hong Kong the opiate blocker naltrexone, which halts any effect from heroin enjoys its best outcomes, as police physically force convicted opiate users to take it every morning. China has 200 'centres for the forcible termination of drug use'. Before the war, police-managed labour camps of this kind were used extensively in America, despite poor outcomes. However, this has not prevented their re-emergence in American drug policy; unrepentant drug users will be forced into army camps to undergo the same training as Marines (Cohen, 1989).

## Softly spoken indoctrination

In Europe drug treatment has liberalised but still concentrates on trying to counter the so-called innate psychological or physiological need for drugs, without reference to social context (Alexander and Hadaway, 1996). The cultural values surrounding drug use are wholly ignored. We have created a social environment where those who are considered to blame for their problems are deemed not to deserve help. As social psychologist John Davies (1993) has observed, this means that what drug users say about themselves is biased in order to elicit credit and deflect blame. Blaming antisocial behaviour on physical compulsions beyond the user's control is particularly appealing. With limited treatment options, over-management of patients by statutory agencies and criminal justice sanctions, it is in the interest of users to conspire with the cultural myth of biological addiction.

Research shows that drug users receive sympathetic responses only if they are trying to change (Schwarzer et al., 1992). This can lead clients to present themselves to services in such a way as to secure treatment elements they want, creating a vast discrepancy with the reality of their lives (Soloway, 1974). Thus how a drug user presents to another user, drug worker, doctor, reporter or judge will vary dramatically, according to need. In court, mugging or burglary may be blamed on unmanageable drug use; in the GP's surgery, continued drug use is blamed on unbearable withdrawal symptoms; while counsellors hear about the troubled lives that users blot out with drugs. When with other users, however, individuals don't present themselves as hopelessly addicted (Davies and Baker, 1987).

The endless repetition of these stories of helplessness only adds to a sense of debilitated self and creates self-fulfilling expectations of loss of control and inability to change. For example, a client of mine was extremely pessimistic that he could change his heroin use as he started on his 12th methadone prescription. I asked him how many times he had actually wanted to stop using heroin in his previous attempts. After long consideration, he confessed that, previously, he had only wanted respite or needed to be seen to be doing something about his use, and had had no intention of stopping. So he had fallen victim to his own hype. Professor William Miller, whose work has revolutionised addiction treatment in recent years, has shown in his research that the expectation of failure is the greatest predictor of failure (Miller and Rollnick, 2002).

## Galileo's children

What happens to the research that does put addiction into a social context? In a shocking and revealing paper, Robert Haskell (1994) of the University of New England, examined the consequences of declaring such research findings and quoted eminent social theorist Alan Marlatt (1983), who pioneered relapse prevention: 'It does not take long for a psychologist or social scientist working in the addiction field to discover that he or she is treading on religious ground and that science and salvation like oil and water do not mix'. His research on social learning and controlled drinking led not only to personal abuse but to the State of Washington passing a law to make controlled-drinker programmes non-reimbursable through state funds.

Haskell suggests the anti-research bias in the field stems from the domination within it of clinicians who themselves have been treated in disease model treatment programmes. But even academics are as guilty. After suggesting in his regular column in an academic addiction journal that controlled drinking was possible, leading addiction expert Stanton Peele was sacked from his column. After publication of his seminal work critiquing the disease model, he was also subjected to personal and professional ridicule. An article published in the *Journal of Psychoactive Drugs* suggested that he wanted a 'stoned American population' and asked whether 'Dr Peele finds something inherently wrong and unappealing about sober consciousness?'

Some of the most vicious comments were reserved for Herbert Fingrette (1988). This notable researcher, whose work had been called upon by the Supreme Court, published a critique, based on empirical data, of alcoholism as a disease. He was subjected to mass harassment. One letter published in the *Los Angeles Times* stated that 'Herbert Fingrette is a disgrace to his profession and should be run out of town on a rail'. In personal correspondence he was described as a 'malignly ignorant man', whilst a former colleague stated in print that 'I worry about the responsibility of a reputable academic press publishing Fingrette's book'.

The correspondent need not worry so much. All of these leading authors had found it extremely difficult to get any work published at all. Even the eminent Professor Thomas Szasz who authored the international classic *Ceremonial Chemistry* (1974), which explored the cultural significance of addictive behaviour, continues to find it enormously difficult to publish his work. Indeed, in fear of funding reprisals from the federal National Institute of Mental Health, the New York State Department of Mental Hygiene tried to sack him. They failed, because of his academic tenure; so they sacked his colleagues instead (Haskell, 1994).

When such researchers do get their work published, there appears to be a mandatory editorial caveat reserved for the expression of counter-ideological views. For instance, the Rand Report (Armour et al., 1978), the findings of which had smashed the Jellinek assumption that controlled drinking was not possible for ex-alcoholics, had its preface amended in subsequent editions to state, 'In particular, *this study does not show that alcoholics may safely resume drinking*, nor does it suggest that any alcoholic should do so' (original italics). This was an attempt to stave off controversy and funding sanctions. In other instances, editors simply overrule their contributors. For example, Norman Zimberg's work on the recreational use of opiates, which was included in the *Handbook on Drug Abuse* (Dupont et al., 1979) was singled out for scathing criticism in the introduction. The Department of Health, Education and Welfare and the National Institute of Drug Abuse, which subscribe to total abstinence, had funded and published the book. Sometimes pro-disease model supporters have simply refused to be published in the same anthologies as these other writers. Entering into an open debate should be essential for the furtherance of any field, yet the personal attacks and informal slandering which have dogged these individuals appear to raise no concern at all. This is even more unjustified in the light of the appalling outcomes of the current stock of treatments (Miller et al., 1995).

## Conclusion

We must accept that we have inherited a vision of addiction from a previous era, characterised by a temperance fantasy of an intoxicant free society. Many of these core assumptions have become enshrined in our thinking, not with the certainty of empirical evidence but on the insistence of a by-gone moral rectitude. Having understood why we think of intoxicants in the way that we do, it is critical we explore the evidence that supports this innate diagnosis of addiction to see if they augment this moral vision, or whether they force us to ask even more questions.

Based on 'The Culture of Cure' *Human Givens: Radical Psychology Today*. Summer 2002

# Chapter 2

# Of Mice and Men

*In fact there was only one species on the planet more intelligent than dolphins, and they spent their time in behavioural research laboratories running round inside wheels and conducting frighteningly elegant and subtle experiments on man. The fact that once again man completely misinterpreted this relationship was entirely according to these creatures' plans.*

Douglas Adams

Tests show pot is as 'addictive as heroin' (Henderson, 2000). This *Times* headline reported a new research finding that squirrel monkeys exposed to THC, one of the psychoactive ingredients in cannabis, were found to self-administer it compulsively. Dr Goldburg, who led the research team, concluded, 'People who want to decriminalise cannabis should look at these findings closely'. This was supported by the UK's anti-drug co-ordinator's office. But the report also stated, 'Previous research always failed to demonstrate that cannabis is addictive in this way'. If the assumption is that mere exposure to cannabis fosters addiction, why did previous exposures not produce similar results?

## Origins of the addicted species

This question goes to the heart of animal studies, a taboo subject in light of obvious ethical concerns. Whilst not supporting animal research, it cannot be ignored whilst the link between animal research and social policy remains extraordinary powerful. WHO (1981) use such tests to calibrate abuse potential and hence legal status of all drugs. This research informs social, cultural, political and treatment values. It is vital that it is questioned rather than allowed to dominate popular thinking but not the open debate. These research studies lend support to the accepted biological 'exposure' thesis. That addiction is determined by a drug's pharmacological action on neurology. Drugs of abuse exert a potent effect on pleasure or pain management sites which elicits euphoric responses in the organism (Nutt, 1996). This positive reinforcing effect spurs the organism to repeat the experience and seek continued gratification, self-administering even to the point of death (Aigner and Balster, 1978). But closer examination of such research reveals a very different picture.

## The nature of nurture

Despite extensive research, it is striking that animals will not self-administer nicotine, tranquillisers or caffeine compulsively, the most frequently abused substances in the Western world (Woods, 1983) but do develop compulsivity for apomorphine, bupropion, procaine and certain antihistamines which do not produce avidity in humans (Balster, 1991). And, whilst outside experimental conditions, animals shun drugs entirely. As Vincent Dole (1980) notes, 'animals generally avoid such drugs when they are given the choice'.

In order to prompt drug consumption, animals are exposed to a range of forces. Typically, subject animals are housed in isolation, in impoverished surroundings with easily available and unlimited supplies of narcotics. Movement is restricted due to the size of the cages and the use of catheters which are a route of administration (Erickson and Alexander, 1989). Falk's (1981) illuminating research observed that animals in laboratory conditions displayed a range of compulsive behaviours even to non-narcotic activities including water consumption, aggression, wheel running and preening amongst others. By careful manipulation of the environment factors, Falk created an ambivalent state of stress in the animals by regulated access to enrichment (food, water, wheel) versus creating a desire to escape the situation (being under body weight). When the opposing attractions of a flight or fight response was equalised, the animal vacillated in obsessive displacement activity whilst waiting for these forces to unbalance and a clear choice could be made. This produced an optimal range of compulsive behaviour, even for consumption of alcohol, where no avidity had been established before. Falk was able to replicate the same patterns of behaviour in humans. Likewise, previous research on monkeys had failed to find cannabis avidity (Woods, 1983). Goldburg's team did not discover the biological attraction of the drug, but the *conditions* which made use compelling. This is a crucial distinction.

## The rat tenements

Alexander et al. (1978, 1998) designed a range of experiments to test the importance of the environmental conditions on consumption. They developed Rat Park, where rats were taught to self-administer oral morphine and placed in distinct environments. One consisted of single pens which housed isolated individuals and the Rat Park itself. This was a large enclosure, 200 times the size of standard lab cages, which replicated the rats' natural environment. Here the gregarious Wister rat lived in groups of 16–20.

The experiment consisted of three phases. Stage one was 'easy access', where rats had access to morphine and a water/quinine solution as bitter as morphine. Both groups shunned morphine and drank water/quinine exclusively. In phase two a 'seduction' technique was employed by increasing the sweetness of the morphine solution every five days, against the second option of pure tap water. In the third phase, described as 'kicking the habit', rats were given morphine solution only for 57 days, then offered a choice between morphine and tap water. In these phases, isolated rats consumed 4–16 times as much morphine as the Rat Park population. Morphine had a negative impact on more fulfilling social interactions for the Rat Park group. Whilst the isolated rats had no other form of stimulation available to them other than the easily accessible morphine. The Rat Park experience suggests compulsive use cannot be construed as an innate action in the personal biochemistry of the organism, but is the individual's response to environmental forces. The reinforcing effect of drugs is magnified or dispelled by the environment (Alexander and Hadaway, 1996).

## Seduction or selection?

Such findings are not limited to the experience of opiates. Peele and DeGrandpre (1998) demonstrated the contextual nature of cocaine consumption. Cocaine appears highly compulsive in impoverished laboratory conditions, but modification of the environment mitigates these levels. When administration is made difficult by increasing the frequency of lever pulling necessary to administer the drug, consumption rates remain steady before tailing off significantly. Rats and monkeys will not increase output for cocaine infusions, suggesting that even at easily accessed levels they are not working as hard they could to administer. Furthermore, in breaking the schedule of availability to alternate hours, consumption rates in monkeys dropped by 75 per cent. They also demonstrate that when alternative reinforcers are introduced, such as banana flavoured food pellets, it dramatically reduced cocaine consumption.

Similar results have been found in human subjects in the area of contingency prescribing. For instance, offering vouchers, on the production of a negative urine sample, for goods such as compact discs or events such as cinema trips or sporting activities has a dramatic effect on compliance and treatment. One research study found that the voucher system reduced positive opiate samples from 80 per cent to 25 per cent amongst methadone maintenance patients (Silverman et al., 1996). Another found it increased abstinence up to 12 weeks for cocaine users, compared to six weeks for those who received only counselling (Higgins et al., 1993, 1994). Furthermore, 75 per cent of the voucher group completed the 24 week programme compared to 40 per cent of the control group. More positive experiences simply crowd out drug use.

## Habit forming

The rate of acquiescence describes how quickly animals acquire compulsive behaviour, and research has highlighted the role of other environmental factors in

conditioning this response. Carroll and Lac (1992) quantified the rate of acquiescence in rats to cocaine over 30 days. In a factorial arrangement, one group of rats
were offered glucose and saccharin solution prior to and during the experiment. A
second received the solution only prior to the experiment whilst the third group
received it during the experiment. The final group received no solution at all.
Extended access to the solution prevented 50 per cent of these rats from developing
acquiescence. Whilst 100 per cent of the water only rats displayed compulsive use
and developed it in the shortest time. Acquiescence was delayed in rats who had
access to glucose solution during the experiment but not prior. A further experiment
was conducted offering not glucose solution but unlimited access to food and again,
25 per cent of the food lavished rats failed to develop compulsive use.

## Appetite for consumption

In terms of appetite, diet and drugs appear to be mutually exchangeable factors in
the consumption rates of all animals. The C57Bl/6J mouse is bred to prefer a 10 per
cent solution of alcohol in preference to tap water. But offered a richer diet of fat
and sugar, they stop even though fluid intake increased three fold. Every study on
alcohol preferring mice has demonstrated this link with consumption and diet (Dole,
1980). Carroll (1993) exposed rhesus monkeys to PCP and water and saccharin
solution which was self-administered through levers. However, the work rate the
animals had to expend to receive either of these solutions was variable. When the
physical cost of saccharin and water were high and PCP was low, the animals
consumed PCP. However when saccharin work rate was lowered, PCP consumption
was reduced by 90 per cent, even when the work demanded was equal or greater
than the expenditure needed to administer PCP. To some degree, the exchange of
one positive reinforcing behaviour for another more readily available one is common
in humans too. The Hall et al. (1989) research suggested that women who did not
gain weight after quitting smoking are more susceptible to relapse. Yung et al.
(1983) found reduced rates of alcohol relapse in men with increased carbohydrate
consumption. Drug users transpose one drug for another when quitting or during
times when the primary drug of choice is in short supply (Alexander and Hadaway,
1996). Compulsivity may be more attractive to us than the objects of our desire.

## Zero tolerance

Tolerance to drugs is typically described as a biological process. This includes
metabolic tolerance which dictates the rate at which the body can break down
drugs. And cellular tolerance which describes the de-sensitisation of the organism's
neurology after continued exposure to drugs. When experiencing environmental
changes, the body must make adjustment to remain within a bandwidth of
functioning. As such, tolerance evolves to compensate for the depressing or

stimulating effect of drugs. However, various researchers highlight that tolerance is determined by psychological and environmental factors (Siegal and Ellsworth, 1986; Poulous and Cappell, 1985; Baker and Tiffany, 1985). Administering opiates in novel settings reduces an animal's tolerance (Siegal and Macrea, 1984). Siegal et al. (1982) developed opiate tolerance in rats in a stable environment. An increased dose was administered to all rats, half in a novel environment. Mortality was 32.4 per cent for rats in a familiar environment, but 64.3 per cent for those in the unfamiliar setting. They surmised that tolerance is dependent on both internal cues of the drugs onset as well as environmental cues associated with administration. Disruption in either field can produce a failure in tolerance with fatal consequences for users. Overdose in humans is a complex process which has all too often been simplified in the media and in drug services. The issue has particular salience for reducing the number of drug related deaths and is explored in more detail in Chapter 3.

## Riders on the storm

Withdrawal is understood as the body's readjustment to the absence of a drug and is allied to tolerance. Whilst the body makes an increasing adjustment for the presence of a drug, as the effect of the substance declines this compensation is no longer counterbalanced. This is known as the law of rebound, which suggests the withdrawal of a drug is the opposite of its effects. But severity remains equally elastic. In an unpublished experiment cited by Davies (1993), three rats in separate cages were yoked together in a network of catheters. The rat in the first pen was able to self-administer morphine. The rat in the second pen passively received a dose every time its stable-mate self administered. The third rat received a dose of Ringer solution. After six days the animals no longer had access to morphine. Only the animals who self-administered morphine displayed withdrawal symptoms. Likewise research on neurotransmission rates found significant biological changes in animals that self-administered as opposed to those that were administered to (Smith et al., 1984; Smith and Dworkin, 1990).

Carroll's (1993) studies observed that symptoms of withdrawal were dependent on environmental conditions. After long term exposure to PCP, abrupt withdrawal was induced in monkeys. However, the work rate necessary for these animals to self-administer food was varied. The animals who received free food displayed the highest levels of withdrawal. Those who had to work to administer food in light of decreasing body weight showed minimal withdrawal. This suggests that withdrawal is connected to psychological forces such as motivation, not purely a biological readjustment post-administration.

Withdrawal symptoms in humans may vary dramatically (Peele, 1998a). In 1929 two researchers, Light and Torrance (1929), tried to index withdrawal symptoms by taking comprehensive biological readings from hospitalised morphine addicts in abrupt withdrawal. Research of this kind could not have been conducted earlier because such a population simply did not exist. They expected to see systematic changes in the addicts' blood, circulation and respiration that would indicate some pattern in the stages of withdrawal. They found that there was no pattern to discern and that the disparate readings that emerged indicated a physiological level of arousal no greater than what one might expect to see in, for instance, team members prior to an important football match. A withdrawal syndrome could not therefore be established, and the researchers concluded that it was only the moaning of the drug users who had gone cold turkey which gave the impression of one. The loudest complainers, however, were the most likely to find relief after injections of a liquid they thought could halt their symptoms but which in fact was sterilised water. Certainly research has demonstrated how the relationship with the prescriber has a significant effect on outcomes in medications, specifically methadone (McCellen et al., 1988). These human factors undermine the purely 'biological event' of withdrawal as an indescribable pain that must be alleviated through continued use.

## No expectations

Withdrawal in individuals with different historical and cultural expectations is very revealing. In the 19th century it was common practice for mothers who worked in factories to sedate their babies all day with opiate compounds as a cheaper alternative to child care. Overdoses were high and led to the introduction of control measures, but doctors did not then observe withdrawal symptoms in these children. They remarked only on the influence of malnutrition and warned of peripheral side effects such as the development of a squint. Meanwhile copious amounts of opiates continued to be given to middle class babies for medical purposes, with no withdrawal symptoms noticed there either (Berridge, 1999).

Today, in the vast majority of new born babes of heroin using mothers, withdrawal is non-existent or undetectable without the 'prior knowledge of maternal addiction', according to the findings of a large American study of over 200 babies (Kron et al., 1975). Another American research team could not identify a single case of withdrawal convulsion in the 198 babies they studied (Ostrea et al., 1975). The vast majority of these babies (94 per cent) showed mild to moderate generalised symptoms of agitation and no medications were necessary. They also found that where symptoms of persistent crying and poor sleep did exist, they were not proportional to the duration or concentration of heroin in the body, as measured in the mother's, child's and the placenta's serum. It does not pay to rely on self-reportage. Most heroin using mothers who do not disclose are not detected without trade mark symptoms such as track marks.

Some new born babies undoubtedly experience difficulties. Kron et al. (1975) conceded 'It is difficult to separate the medical complications caused by long term *in utero* narcotic exposure of the infant from those generated by the multiple health problems of the addicted mother'. Infant 'withdrawal' does correlate with low birth weight and other metabolic imbalances. And the reappearance of symptoms in infants suggests that there is more permanent damage caused by the impurities in the heroin used in pregnancy and the poor pre-natal lifestyle of the mother.

It has also been suggested that abnormal behaviour in this small group is the result of the mothers' difficulty in establishing maternal bonds with their children (Coppolillo, 1975). Besides the mother's drug usage, depression and guilt which interferes with this process, mother and baby are often separated by clinicians during this critical early period. Such bonds play an essential role in babies' development (Kegan, 1982). Taking a wider perspective, it is far too simplistic to reduce this infant trauma to a single factor of narcosis alone.

## High expectations

Alternatively, the role of placebo in modifying mood is well established and challenges the biomedical determinism of addiction. Placebo alcohol can produce sexual arousal, increased aggression and cravings for more alcohol, while disguised alcohol can often not induce any of these effects (Bridwell et al., 1978; Lang et al., 1975; Marlatt et al., 1991). There are also compelling positive placebo results for treating anxiety, dementia, depression, panic disorders, schizophrenia and pain relief to degrees which rival or exceed medical interventions (Dixon and Sweeney, 2000). Walach's (2003) review of studies also identified that placebo effects were powerful mediators that could equal or outperform medications. Placebo effects were highly dependent on context of administration, being both the products of habituation as well as expectation. For example, when subjects in research programmes were informed that the active drug to placebo ratio was high, 16:1, placebo effects were amplified as the subject become more confident they would receive the active medication on the balance of probability. The effects of placebo are not a purely psychological artefact, but can promote neurological changes in the brain (Leuchter et al., 2002). Active placebo, that induces side effects, can have even greater effects on the body, as the physical sensation enhances the idea that the drug is doing something.

## Elements of disgust

Drugs are not purely placebo and do have an objective effect on the body. Drugs alter the metabolism yet many of the mechanisms by which they do this are not understood. However, this disruption does not reveal its nature to the user, instead they must interpret and evaluate the kind of experience that they are having. These evaluations are based on subjective expectations which are situated within the cultural world view which they occupy. Hence, whilst street users report a preference for heroin over methadone, they cannot distinguish them in a Pepsi-cola style challenge (McMurran, 1997). Whilst users in one study estimated heroin purity in the locality as anywhere between 20–80 per cent (cf. Winn, 2001). Step into other cultures or sub-cultures and we see strikingly different behaviours on drugs and alcohol. For example, if we consider the behaviour of Western drinkers such as elated mood, increased sexual interest, sociability and confidence, none of these are pharmacological properties of the drug. Chronic opiate use now qualifies us for sickness benefit, yet the great industrial achievements of the Victorian canal and rail network were built by navvies sedating their exertion with opiates. Likewise, what we witness in withdrawal is the restoration of the body's natural homeostasis after a drug no longer distorts its metabolism. But how the experience is interpreted and amplified is essentially a psycho-cultural drama of expectations. Emotional responsiveness, which had been suppressed by drug use, may be the most difficult aspect of this process, along with the deep anxiety of feeling unable to cope with a despairing life. Hence street users and hospital patients having very different experiences of withdrawal from opiate based pain killers.

We can liken this process to the evolution of disgust. There is no innately disgusting response in human beings, but the evolution of such cultural expectancies can be charted in children. Under the right conditions, presentation of a disgusting stimulus will provoke violent biological reactions and anxiety but this is driven by learned cultural norms, not biology. Research which supports this cultural perspective has shown, through brain scanning imagery, that neurochemical changes in the brain in drug dependent people are triggered by memory rather than key receptors in the brain or pleasure centres (cf. Booth, 1997).

Although the range of pharmacological solutions to the 'problem' of craving has increased, none of these treatments is free standing but is always sold in the small print as an adjunct to psychosocial counselling programmes. Results from using pharmacological aids alone have been disappointing in the long term, even if successful to some degree in the short term. Unfortunately users tend to ascribe early success to the drug, not themselves, and so don't build up confidence in their own efforts. Pharmaceutical companies are even investing in counselling research to give themselves an edge in a lucrative market (Prochaska (undated), Archives of Canada).

## Primed candidates

Animal behavioural research has attempted to provide cogent models in regards to relapse. Once regular drug administration is stopped, a small priming shot of the narcotic can prompt compulsive use once again, but only when primed by the drug the animal was previously exposed too (Marlatt, 1996). Once again, relapse is triggered by starving the animals of positive reinforcers such as food (Carroll and Comer, 1996) and re-administrating in the same environment that housed the previous drug episode (Robson, 1999). Relapse animal studies are limited (Carroll and Comer, 1996; Miller, 1996). Re-administration of a priming dose is not a choice made by the animal, because even after long term narcotic exposure animals prefer food (Marlatt, 1996). Relapse models raise the most critical issue in animal research reliability in explaining human addiction. Animals do not operate under cultural expectations like humans which have a significant role in whether a lapse triggers full relapse into uncontrolled use. Individuals who ascribe lapses to innate factors beyond their control appear at higher risk of relapse than those who ascribe lapse to external factors than can be managed (Curry et al., 1987).

## Exposure assumption

Overemphasis on biology has produced a narrow repertoire of pharmacological responses to the addictive experience but with limited success. Dole and Nyswander (1976), who developed methadone treatment for the metabolic problem of heroin addiction, have since recognised that methadone's results have been disappointing. Today, methadone is predominately used as a means of weaning people off illicit opiates in reduction regimes. The UK's National Treatment Outcomes Research Study, which monitors treatment effectiveness, found that after six months 59 per cent of patients on methadone reduction programmes were still receiving treatment – only eight per cent less than those on maintenance prescriptions (Ashton, 1999). In clinical practice, whilst the demand for methadone remains high, outcomes remain poor as the 'cure'.

## Conclusion

Animal behavioural research cannot be understood to support the biological origins of addiction whilst it remains dependant upon the environmental conditions to elicit the compulsive range of behaviours. Sadly, its findings have been taken purely at face value and imported into human models of addiction, which continue to view addiction outside of the contexts it occurs in. As a result, the current stock of low intensity interventions fails to address the range of the human experience if it focuses solely on removing the need for drugs from the individual, either biologically or psychologically. Treatment remains frozen in our current situation, where biological sciences continue to provide answers but no solutions. Having explored the defining concepts of biological addiction in animals we must now transpose these findings onto human subjects and evaluate how these broader forces affect the human experience of drug taking, other than the purely physical action of drugs.

# Chapter 3

# The Myth of Overdose

*That is what we fear-no sight no sound,*
*No touch no taste or smell, nothing to think with,*
*Nothing to love or link with,*
*The anaesthetic from which none come round.*

Philip Larkin

If we apply the biological issues to human experiences we find more complexities than our biological preoccupations can explain. With government setting targets to reduce opiate related deaths, overdose itself has come to the foreground in the drugs field. It has been estimated that approximately one per cent of the heroin using population will die as a result of overdosing. Studies show that 23 to 33 per cent of heroin injectors had experienced non-fatal overdose in the previous twelve months, whilst 68 per cent had a non-fatal experience within their heroin using career (Ruttenber and Luke, 1984; Gossop et al., 1996; Taylor et al., 1996). Attempts to curb this tragic loss of life are welcome, but the latest government targets raise critical issues in how overdose can be abated. Whilst the explanations of overdose have become widely accepted, if we investigate the reality closely we are confronted with perplexing challenges which are not easily resolved.

## 'Classic' overdose

Current thinking assumes that overdose is caused through exposure to high levels of heroin. The drug operates on three receptor sites in the brain which are responsible for analgesia, euphoria and respiration amongst other effects (Julien, 1998). After intravenous injection, 68 per cent of the heroin crosses the blood-brain barrier in 15–20 seconds. It is heroin's suppressing action on respiratory receptor sites that causes coma, respiratory failure and as a result, death (Drake and Zadar, 1996). 'Classic' overdose is assumed to be especially pertinent with doses of heroin which exceed acquired physical tolerance. It is believed that periods of abstinence, followed by pre-abstinence levels of re-administration, or exceptionally pure heroin, exceeds acquired tolerance. Nearly all studies show overdose rates are primarily amongst injectors. In one study (Gossop et al., 1996) only two out of 125 non-injectors reported experience of non-fatal overdose whilst there has only been one recorded death through oral administration (Sporer, 1999).

Within the field this explanation of overdose is widely accepted. And practitioners are wise to inform their clients of the obvious risks suggested by this research. However, there are problems inherent in this explanation. The full nature of overdose is only partially represented and other risks are neglected, placing clients in even greater danger. If we wish to address the issues of overdose we must confront these inadequacies in our current understanding in order to minimise the risks undoubtedly posed.

## 'Underdose'

As Brecher (1972) has pointed out, the purity of street heroin has been in decline since the 1940s, when overdose was virtually unknown, compared to today when overdose rates have soared. Furthermore, when we look at individuals who experience overdose, all studies confirm that the vast majority are long term users, not novice users who would be expected to be at greater risk due to lower tolerance (see Grund, 1993). Reviewing current literature Darke et al. (1996) surmised that, 'Contrary to popular belief, the "typical" overdose victim is not a young novice or inexperienced user. Rather, the average age of death reported is in their late twenties and early thirties.' One study (Zadar et al., 1996) identified that only 17 per cent of deaths were attributable to novice or recreational users.

Humans can withstand very high doses of opiates. Research by Kolb and Mez (1931) estimated that an opiate naive individual can withstand doses of up to 500 mg of pure heroin. Other research studies have placed the figure between 200 mg (Driesbach, 1971) and up to 350 mg (Salter, 1959). Opiate tolerant users can administer far higher doses. The Light and Torrance (1929) research in the 1920s found that users consumed up to 1,680 mg. One subject was injected with 1,800 mg over a two and a half hour period and did not show signs of sickness. Furthermore, dramatic increases in dose did not increase the risk of overdose. In the same study opiate users were administered up to nine times their normal dose without measurable changes in metabolic rates. In the 1960s pilot methadone trials conducted by Dole and Nyswander, they administered subjects with 200 mg of heroin in one dose. These patients showed no physical signs of respiratory depression (cf. Brecher, 1972). These are enormous doses compared to the purity levels of street heroin.

As Siegel et al. (1982) noted, whilst some people do die of high dosage, autopsy reports consistently reveal that, '. . . many experienced drug users die after a dose that should not be fatal in view of their tolerance. Indeed some die following a heroin dose that was well tolerated the previous day.' Research (Davoli et al., 1993) has indicated that the 12 months post rehabilitation and the first two weeks after release from prison (Seaman et al., 1998) are high risk periods for overdose. But Brecher's (1972) findings suggest that even after a period of abstinence, heroin consumption levels in these cases is often so low that they cannot account for overdose. Analysis of heroin in the body, syringes and packets very rarely indicate abnormally high levels of purity. Furthermore, heroin users tend to use in group settings but it is ex-tremely rare for more than one individual to overdose. This also dispels the assumption that overdose is caused by toxic adulterants in the heroin itself, which is rarely found to be the case too. In light of this evidence it is important that we ask what are the real contributory factors in these deaths?

## Polydrug use

One of the biggest factors in overdose related deaths is the presence of other drugs. When heroin is used alongside other central nervous depressants, it amplifies the overall effect on the respiratory system, regardless of the route heroin is adminis-tered (Sporer, 1999). The prime candidates are alcohol, barbiturates and tranquil-lisers, though other studies have also indicated ecstasy and cocaine can contribute to overdose (Taylor et al., 1996). Research studies have identified that 27 per cent (Zadar et al., 1996) to 70 per cent (Darke et al., 1996) of people used other drugs alongside heroin at the time of fatal and non-fatal overdose. This is supported by Brecher's historical analysis of changing trends in consumption since 1940, when heroin addicts were once deeply antithetical to the use of alcohol: an attitude which has since changed.

The understanding of the interactions of polydrug use is an important area. Heroin is no greater a contributory factor to overdose than the other drugs consumed, but all overdoses are invariably reported as heroin overdoses in the media. Deaths from multiple drug use can cause respiratory failure but also precipitate other risk factors, for example asphyxiation on vomit whilst sleeping. Peele has analysed media reporting on clusters of assumed heroin purity overdoses. In New York 'purer' heroin allegedly claimed 14 lives. What emerged was that two of these people died of natural causes, four were cocaine related alone and all but one of the remaining eight were polydrug users (Peele, 1994). Whilst of the four deaths in the Texas cluster, three were caused by choking on vomit not overdose (Peele, 1998b). Initial press reports were not amended. Misrepresentation of the real risks of polydrug use by focusing on heroin may only succeed in placing more lives in unnecessary danger.

## Syndrome X

But there are still some more difficult issues raised regarding the actual causes of death. It takes several hours to die from a heroin overdose (Sporer, 1999). This has led many to campaign for the opiate blocker, Naloxone, to be offered to all heroin users in a take home form (Darke and Hall, 1997). As up to 85 per cent of overdoses happen in group settings this could vastly reduce the number of heroin related deaths (Sporer et al., 1996). Yet in some heroin related deaths, onset is so rapid that the victim is found with the needle still in the vein and autopsy reveals that heroin has not reached the brain tissues. This does not suggest heroin poisoning but a sudden toxic shock reaction, what Brecher (1972) describes as 'Syndrome X'. Death may also be caused by a massive pulmonary oedema, the lungs flooding with water. Other autopsies have identified brain oedema as the cause of death. Besides water in the brain there is also fragmentation in the astrocyte cells, perhaps caused by the repeated injection of crude adulterants. Such conditions appear to be exacerbated by the combination of drugs, again alcohol and tranquillisers in particular.

## Anti-tolerance

Whilst purity, adulteration, periods of abstinence and polydrug use offer important contributions to the understanding of heroin related deaths, they do not provide a complete explanation. Research shows that not all heroin users take multiple substances. They have high tolerance with no periods of abstinence but still overdose, whilst methadone reduces the risk of overdose (Sporer, 1999). In order to understand this mystery we must revise our understanding of the processes of tolerance. Tolerance is typically described as a metabolic process (how fast the body can breakdown a substance) and a cellular process (where brain receptors become desensitised by the repeated action of drugs). However, it appears the tolerance is developed in response to the psycho-cultural factors surrounding the drug use (Siegel et al., 1982). (See Chapter 2.)

A host of research studies on mammals have consistently highlighted this process (for overview see Baker and Tiffany, 1985). In one experiment, rats were administered heroin and then placed on a warm plate. The number of times the rat licks its paw indexes the pain killing effect of heroin and at what level. Building up rats' tolerance in one environment, then administering the drug in a new environment, reduced the analgesic effect of the drug (Adams et al., 1969). This indicates that rats' expectations and anticipations have a direct effect on the metabolism, in preparation to compensate for the administration of the drug. Environmental and cognitive cues trigger this 'counter-response' to anticipated exposure creating higher tolerance. Research has demonstrated disruption of these environmental cues reduces tolerance for amphetamine (Carlton and Wolgin, 1971; Poulos et al., 1981), scopolamine (Poulos and Hinson, 1984), alcohol (Pinel et al., 1985), barbiturates (Wahlstrom, 1968), heroin (Rochford and Stewart, 1987) and naloxone (Greeley et al., 1988) amongst others. But is this tolerance enough to insulate against overdose?

These situational factors surrounding drug consumption have a dramatic impact on tolerance for a host of drugs including alcohol. This experience is most familiar as the 'dinner party effect' where we can consume large amounts of alcohol at home without feeling inebriated but get intoxicated on far lower volumes in unfamiliar settings. Likewise, daytime drinking has a more potent effect when it departs from an established drinking pattern of evening use.

This experience translates to heroin use. This places opportunistic users who use in public places, often the nearest available location to their supplier, at very high risk. In Cabramatta, a district in Sydney, an increase in heroin street selling saw the number of heroin related deaths rise dramatically. In 1995, 10 per cent of heroin related deaths in Sydney were found in street settings, in Cabramatta 90 per cent of deaths were in street settings. Again, heroin purity could not account for these deaths and yet this was widely publicised by the police and the media (see Bammer and Sengoz, 1995).

A preoccupation with purely biological mechanisms of drug use means that vulnerable people are not being alerted to the real dangers. High risks groups such as people leaving prison, treatment programmes, poly users and the homeless are prone to find themselves using in novel settings. Every research programme has found these groups to be at significantly higher risk of overdose. In one study in Hamburg, homeless users accounted for over a third of all deaths. This risk is amplified by the effects of poverty on health and mood which also appear to be contributing factors. Users in social groups of high deprivation are over six times more likely to overdose than those in more affluent economic groups (cf. Report by the Advisory Council on the Misuse of Drugs, 2000).

Whilst 'contingent' tolerance has been explained through Pavlovion conditioning (Siegel and Ellsworth, 1986), habituation (Baker and Tiffany, 1985) and homeostatic theory (Poulos and Cappell, 1985), researchers largely agree that there are two sets of triggers which initiate this tolerance counter-response. The first are environmental conditions including the setting, preparation and other sensory queues. The second trigger is stimulated in the mind of the user by the signals of the drug taking effect (Siegel et al., 1982). If these cues are disrupted, by drug use in an alien environment, or effects distorted by the action of another drug, this can produce a 'failure' in expectation, drastically compromising acquired tolerance. The result is a classic overdose syndrome in a drug user with otherwise high tolerance. Siegel and Macrae (1984) reported that 'In interviews with a number of human "overdose" survivors, the majority of respondents reported that the circumstances of the drug administration were atypical on the occasion of the overdose, that is, the usual drug-associated cues were not present when the "overdose" occurred.'

The environmental specificity of tolerance places key groups of drug users at risk. Opportunistic/multiple users, homeless people and those leaving treatment/prison are likely to find themselves using in very different environments to previous settings. People reduce the risk of overdose by following a clear routine of administration in an environment they associate with drug use, without disrupting internal expectancies with other psychoactive drugs. These environments can be very specific. Research indicates that overdoses do happen in the home, however, and a case study of a terminally ill patient on morphine demonstrates how minor changes can have a dramatic impact on tolerance (Siegel and Ellsworth, 1986). The patient was administered over 100 shots of morphine, in his bedroom. The day he died of classic morphine poisoning though he was administered the same dosage but in his sitting room.

## Conclusion

If we are sincere in our hope to reduce the tragic loss of life it is important we have a clear understanding of the real risks posed and what can be done to limit them. The Australian Nation Research Centre warns, 'Both heroin users and service providers need to be disabused of the myth that heroin overdoses are solely, or even mainly, attributable to fluctuations in heroin purity' (cf. Peele, 1998b). With overdose rates continuing to soar, the UK government's own report states, 'drug related deaths are often casually embedded in complicated and as yet not fully understood nexus of adverse social context' (Report by the Advisory Council on the Misuse of Drugs, 2000). The real dangers lie in consumption of drugs along with alcohol, not just heroin. It is also about lifestyle, the social and environmental context and ignorance of the real dangers. Unless we can address this wider spectrum of the drug using experience we may do little to reduce the number of needless deaths. And as everyone who has experienced a loss through drug related death knows, that is simply not good enough. But what we also observe here is that the drug using experience cannot be reduced to a discrete biological event located in the user. The defining features of the experience are contingent upon the individual's relationship with their environment, not just pharmacological actions on the brain. We must now broaden the scope of these considerations and explore the idea of addiction itself, and whether it too can be understood as a purely biological issue or whether its influence reaches further than is currently imagined.

An edited version of this article appeared as 'The Myth of Overdose', *Addiction Today* March 2001. Additional material from the 'Lethal Underdose', *Bizarre* November 2001 (52)

# Chapter 4

# Engineering Genetics

*Science becomes dangerous only when it imagines that it has reached its goal.*
George Bernard Shaw

The genetic focus on addiction cultivates the common credo that compulsive behaviours are essentially a hereditary disease. This idea has been received with obvious sympathy from treatment ideologies that were already convinced addiction was a progressive and intractable disease, yet lacked any causal explanation. However, despite huge investment of both money and scientific talent, reviewing the developments from this field erode the very position it has hoped to maintain. How robust is this assumption and what will genetics offer us in the field of addiction treatment?

## Origins of the speculation

It was not until the 20th century that the rubric of DNA was unravelled and in the unwinding tumbled out a vast mythology of this molecule. In reality, DNA is a large but inert molecule. It does not replicate itself but depends wholly on the organelles of the cell. Likewise DNA does not produce proteins, but provides the information for the cell machinery to build proteins. And a vast interplay of genes (alleles) are responsible, not single ones. Not only do we inherit our parental genetic material, we inherit the cell machinery too.

Almost 45 per cent of human DNA is junk, subsumed from viruses and bacteria. Interspersed within this are a paltry 30,000 genes, 300 more than the mouse. During the transposing of information from DNA a host of variables enter into play. Subtle environmental effects called 'interference' impact on the developing embryo, causing the asymmetry in organisms for instance. The machinery makes mistakes in the copy editing, producing random mutation. It is the sum measure of these weak and unpredictable forces which ultimately determine the expression of DNA, rather than the absolute authority of the molecule expressing its dread command (Hubbard and Wald, 1993). As Kitcher (1997) points out, geneticists are all too apt at using an over-simplified short hand regarding the expression of multiple genes, omitting '. . . in a standard environment'. Environmental forces can shut the action of genes on or off. A change in environment can change the expression of genes.

## A matter of breeding

Within the realm of the genetic origins of addiction several methods have been devised to support this position. Primary among genetic studies has been the selective breeding of laboratory animals. We have already encountered the C57Bl/6J mice, bred to prefer a 10 per cent solution of alcohol in preference to tap water. Blood plasma testing demonstrates that although these genetically predisposed animals consumed alcohol when available it was not at sufficient levels to induce inebriation. By manipulation of environmental factors Falk's (1981) rats were 'legally drunk night and day'. Despite continued efforts, the instigator of methadone Vincent Dole (1980) concludes, 'The classic procedure of selective breeding to generate strains that like beverage-concentration alcohol in their diet does not appear to have produced animals that seek alcohol for its pharmacological effect.'

## The human gene-no

Within the human species the hunt has been on for the addictive gene and has proved as elusive as a junky mouse. Blum and Payne's (1992) research, trumpeted as the genetic breakthrough in understanding alcoholism, identified a defective D2 dopamine receptor gene in 69 per cent of 70 alcoholic cadavers. Follow up research studies failed to find a significant link between the gene and alcoholism. A meta-analysis of all study results indicates that the defective gene frequency was 0.18 across alcoholic, problematic and non-alcoholic populations alike (Peele, 1992, 1995b).

'Neuro-genetic' research, observing the action of neuro-transmitters such as dopamine on receptor sites in the brain, opens up three central problems. Firstly, neuro-transmitters play a multifaceted role in the brain making it impossible to see why a defect would only produce one specific abnormal behaviour—addiction (Breggin, 1993). Secondly, some drugs like heroin operate on specific receptor or transporter sites whilst others operate globally on the brain like alcohol. No mechanism which can account for these diverse mechanisms producing one outcome has been identified. Whilst mice that have been genetically modified devoid of neuro-transporter sites associated with the action of drugs such as cocaine, display the same behaviours as their genetically unmodified counterparts in chamber preference experiments (NIDA Press Release, 1998). Thirdly, neuro-transmission rates can vary in long term drug users (again not conclusively), but this does not proceed exposure (Dean, 1997). Whilst we have seen self-administration plays a vital role in these transmission rates, rather than the presence of the drug per se (see Chapter 2). This suggests a more complex role for cognition and expectation driving neuro-chemistry rather than vice versa. This is supported by brain imaging. It is easy to forget that neurological sites in these subjects' brains are not being stimulated by the action of the drug but purely by invoked memory through images of use or paraphernalia.

If we look at the macro-picture of drug consumption we also see important cultural divergence, inexplicable within a genetic framework. Whilst the objective effects of drugs on the brain remain constant, the subjective effects of drugs mean that different cultures, sub-cultures and even age ranges experience them very differently, leading to a diverse range of behaviour, even on the very same drug. Furthermore, compulsive use like alcoholism is virtually unknown in Mediterranean countries despite high alcohol consumption. Irish Americans are seven times more likely to become addicted than those of Mediterranean descent, and Jewish communities show negligible rates of addiction (Peele, 1990). France has a high consumption rate of alcohol and attendant alcoholism. But this population displays none of the psychopathology associated with the equally high consumption rates of Taiwan (O'Brien and McClellan, 1996). The Sahal bushmen of Niger experience problematic consumption of tea and sugar (Klien, 2001). Whilst 'pica', eating inanimate matter, is a common compulsion in aboriginal cultures (Falk, 1983). The highly diverse consumption patterns and behavioural responses to drugs is well documented, and cannot be accounted for within a deterministic genetic framework as the genome shows that race is a social not biological construct (Angier, 2000). Genetic difference may account for varying sensitivities to alcohol as in the case of 'oriental flush' in Asian populations. Genetically, this population is unable to produce an enzyme which breaks down alcohol leading to a high sensitivity to both alcohol's effects and hangovers. However, whilst the Native American Indian and Inuit experience this genetic defect and the highest rates of alcoholism in the US, so too do the Chinese and Japanese populations that experience the lowest rates of alcoholism in the US. Increased genetic susceptibility to alcohol's effects does not translate into alcoholism.

## Oliver Twist reality

Without an addiction gene materialising, much has been made of twin studies as the proof of inheritance. Again, findings for such studies have proved indecisive. Some studies find a correlation but others do not, with researchers finding a wide degree of variance in their estimations. Vaillant's (1995) longitudinal study of alcoholism across life span, found that 27 per cent of those born to an alcoholic parent did develop alcoholism, as opposed to five per cent amongst those with difficult childhoods but no alcoholic parent. However, this also demonstrates that 73 per cent did not develop problems at all despite alcoholic relatives and that those without a family history were also prone. Furthermore, his research suggested that the earlier onset of alcoholism in males had a much poorer prognosis for treatment success, which is an important issue we will explore in Chapter 6. However, this group showed the least correlation with parental alcoholism (onset at 29.2 years); whilst the high genetically correlated group drank problematically much later (onset at 40.1 years) and had the best treatment outcomes. So, taking this research purely at face value, in terms of extended quality of life and treatment outcomes you would appear better off with a genetic disposition. Ultimately, Vaillant concluded that on an individual basis, children of alcoholic parentage were as likely to become teetotal as they were to be alcoholics.

Variance in prevalence rates has dogged all genetic research of behaviour. For example, over a hundred years of research into the inheritability of I.Q. has not produced any conclusive results. Plotkin (2002) suggests this may be accounted for as an error in assessing the inheritance of a mechanism over a process. It is one thing to access functioning of a tangible mechanism, like a sample of the liver to reveal its ability to produce an enzyme. Where mechanisms have structural problems they are readily identifiable, it can be seen, measured and touched as in the case of organic brain damage. But there is no central organelle in the body that produces 'intelligence' as there is no addiction 'centre' in the brain producing 'addictiveness'. Whilst the apparatus of the human brain is inherited, we cannot inherit these processes. We do not speak English because we are born with a larynx the same as parents. Dr Craig Venter (2001), head of the private genome project, highlighted the central role of human processes in regards to cloning. Despite identical genomes, and because of life experience he estimates the odds of two clones having two identical personalities are 'close to zero'. Processes are defuse, on going interactions between the organism and its environment which, as Wahlsten and Gottieleb (1997) suggest, cannot be definitively attributed to genetics unless a major gene(s) is identified. No addiction gene has yet been forthcoming. So much of human behaviour is process driven and changes over time, where alcohol and drug consumption varies dramatically over life's course. The comparison of an older generation parents' consumption, which could be due to later onset of alcoholism, to the sibling in the adolescence, where consumption is demographically high for this social group, would produce a high correlation that would not necessarily endure over a subsequent ten year period.

This does not discount the weaker secondary effects of genes, for example extroverts appear to show higher problematic experiences of substance misuse not as an inevitable biological deficiency but as a failure to respond to negative social punishments which self-correct antisocial behaviour. Or gene operations being switched on or off by environmental triggers. But in either scenario we witness a confluence of interactions which are not predetermined by genes alone.

Twin studies themselves are not immune from criticism. Twins are not separated at birth for the benefit of geneticists, and many subjects are brought up by extended family in the same neighbourhoods (Lewontin, 2000). Whilst Kamin (1977, 1995) also revealed that many twin test subjects who were apparently separated had spent extensive time together prior to research and ensuing publicity allowed them to sell their 'special twin bond' story to a media ever hungry for human interest stories. The *selective placement* of adoption may also place these children in similar environment-al conditions as their separated sibling. For those raised in care, sexual abuse revelations have become a shocking norm, whilst foster families can prove as dysfunctional as any other family unit. A wide spectrum of specialist support agencies exists for care leavers who experience higher rates of social problems, regardless of their parents' usage. As such, both parents and offspring may experience problems within their own social milieu but for completely different reasons other than genetic. The fact that they may be addicted to different drugs, which act in completely different ways on the brain is also an inexplicable factor within our current understanding. Currently it is difficult to understand how one inherited abnormality might explain two different and contradictory chemical predispositions in related individuals, or why one individual may become addicted to two very contradictory substances. As maverick psychiatrist Thomas Szaz (1974) has pointed out, pharmacology is to addiction as gynaecology is to having sex.

Rarely have these studies taken into consideration the vast cultural differences within the populations they study which may significantly skew the results. In calculating risk factors of developing problematic consumption, Sutherland's (2004) research suggests that those with a biological parent who is addicted are twice as likely to develop an addiction, but unaccounted cultural difference could reduce this further. Whilst those 'raised' rather than 'sired', in a household with a problematic user of alcohol or drugs are nine and twelve times more likely of developing alcohol and drug problems respectively. Within 'un-separated' families, Harding (2000) noted that whilst the offspring raised by problematic users do have a greater probability of problematic consumption, equally so do the offspring of teetotal parents. One group fails to learn the unacceptable threshold of consumption whilst the former learns no skills in managing intoxicants. This also serves to dismiss the reverse logic that those without high addiction rates within their family tree might use drugs and alcohol with impunity.

## Gene genies

Much of the interest in genetics lies in the hope of developing effective pharmacological treatments to curtail addictive behaviours. Whilst this is a noble enterprise we must remember that no successful gene replacement therapy yet exists. Gains have been made in treating genetic illnesses by identifying the protein deficits in patients, as in the case of the degenerative Huntingdon's disease. Without treatment sufferers would die in early adolescence. But this simply does not fit the pattern we see in addiction. People sustain abstinence without recourse to pharmacological support and are none the worse for it. The vast majority cease use without any treatment. Pharmacological optimism appears to lie in the production of 'neuro-genetic' drugs which will halt cravings and thus prevent relapses. Yet the existence of preventative opiate, alcohol and nicotine medications have proved of little long term efficacy. Even those receiving pharmaceuticals of choice do not seem to prosper. In the area of heroin addiction, we have seen that the prescribing of substitute methadone has not been as transformative as insulin is to diabetics. Whilst research into prescribing heroin found 12 per cent of subjects sold their supply on (Hartnoll et al., 1980). These medications would theoretically serve to compensate for any alleged neuro-genetic deficit. But one cannot imagine Huntingdon patients behaving in such a way.

The promise of a new age of anti-anxiety drugs to halt cravings has the hallmark of potential disaster. There is no physiological link yet established between drug use and cravings, but we do know that every anxiety relieving drug currently available has the capacity to elicit compulsive use. We forget that morphine was devised to wean people off opium, heroin to wean people off morphine and methadone to wean people off heroin. If a drug was developed that could wholly eliminate any negative consequences of use or cessation, in reality, this may have the opposite effect. The lack of consequences would make picking up a drug and using again *more* attractive, not less, unless the individual showed a very high degree of self-motivation. Certainly this was indicated in trials of buprenorphine (Law et al., 1997).

## The long and winding code

Mapping the genome is a major step forward in our understanding of molecular biology. But because of the influence of multiple genes inferred in illnesses, a much wider bank of genetic subjects is needed for comparison before illness can be understood. What is striking about its initial findings is the small number of genes available to humans: a fact that disturbed the possibility of lucrative markets inducing some pharmaceutical companies to demand a recount. There is simply not enough genetic material to go around and compensate for the variations witnessed in human behaviour. As Venter (2001) warned, 'There are two fallacies to be avoided. Determinism, the idea that all characteristics of a person are "hard wired" by the genome; and reductionism, that now the human sequence is completely known it is a matter of time before our understanding of gene functions and interactions will provide a complete causal description of variability.' His rival, Dr Francis Collins (2001) echoed this sentiment almost to the word. The question appears to be not why are humans genetically programmed but instead, why do genes exert such little influence over human behaviour compared to other species?

Within a broader reproductive framework it would appear that Mother Nature deploys two key reproductive strategies. Animals with a short lifespan have a rapid breeding cycle where they produce masses of offspring who are reliant on a blueprint of behaviours (Plotkin, 2002). Their short lifespan precludes learning, but through genetic variations each offspring is relatively well adapted or not to the environment. In sudden environmental change, the slight variation will favour a percentage of these offspring that will survive and pass on their fitness. Humans produce very few offspring. We have a breeding cycle in excess of twenty years. A huge amount of environmental change can occur within this time frame. To be limited to a blueprint of behaviours would render us environmentally obsolete before maturation. To compensate we have the most complex organ in the animal kingdom: the human brain. It is so large that we are born 11 months premature otherwise we could not pass through the birth canal. It consumes 20 per cent of oxygen and glucose at rest (Leaky, 1994). Much of its neural architecture is shaped by the world it inhabits. It is this sensitivity to its environment that allows us to adapt and thrive as a species. We call this adaptability human intelligence. Plotkin (2000) suggests that only the most basic of actions such as reflexes are programmed in. The capacity for language too, being able to conceptualise the world and transmit meaning to others. We can frame and pool our adaptations with others of our species creating a collective bank of knowledge called culture. Humans live in a cultural world of concepts, beliefs and associations not a natural one of brute survival. Here is the richness of human behaviour. It is because we are not limited to a strict blueprint of behaviours that makes us the most flexible species in the world. No other species can live in the Sahara or Antarctic. And no other species can make use of its environment as we do. We shape and are shaped by it; where we fail to do so we suffer. Our capacity to thrive is also our capacity to despair.

## Politics in the blood

There is a critical point in genetic studies whilst not immediately salient to the addiction field is important none the less. In the study of genetics one fact remains inescapable in the literature. Genetics is a politic view. Whilst so much of the high sciences have remained aloof from the affairs of man, genetics remains the most controversial and politically charged physical science. This reaches beyond the ethics of cloning but strikes a much deeper chord in the Western imagination. The root of this is a deep cultural obsession with individualism. As if individualism is possible in a mass production/consumption society. Since Western populations swung towards ever greater degrees of mass conformity, it seemed to necessitate an ever increasing sense of ourselves as especially particular.

In the West we need only consider that there has been a gene suggested for all social ills, from crime, drug use, mental health, obesity, unemployment and even homelessness, to understand the political utility in such a position. Like the philosopher Liebnitz's claim that this is 'the best possible of worlds' it breeds a resignation to an established 'market led' political order that these problems are located in individuals rather than the result of the social organisation. Even today, genetics continues to promote right wing agendas as rabid as the days of eugenics. Herrnstein and Murray's (1994) *The Bell Curve*, promoted the concept of racial inferiority of intelligence, whilst Rushton's (1995) *Race, Evolution and Behaviour* and Brand's (1996) *The g Factor*, have propagated even more radical racist right wing agendas. Brand's book was removed from sale when he confessed that he was 'perfectly proud to be a racist in a scientific sense' (Gross et al., 1997). Genetics and politics can never be divorced whilst the science is used to justify the inequities of the social order that pays its research grants.

## Conclusion

Brunner (1990) suggests modern society has come to blame the body for addiction as it is not making moral decisions; thus rendering the antisocial behaviours more tolerable than treatable. But the gratification of the moral majority may condemn the drug using minority to self-defeat as the price of that understanding. Historically, the medicalisation of addiction did much to legitimatise and de-stigmatise treatment. However, the deterministic expectations that it implied, and which are enshrined in genetic research, may have a negative impact on any treatment success. Many problematic users present for services convinced they have an intractable genetic disorder that erodes their belief in the capacity for change. Numerous research studies have all identified that expectations play a huge role in recovery, and that those who attribute compulsive use to innate factors beyond their control exhibit far higher and more prolonged rates of relapse (Marlatt, 1996). What is important is not to dismiss genetics entirely from the equation of human nature, but to recognise that even within our current understanding genetic *inheritability* does not translate into genetic *inevitability*.

Genetics elicits the hope that science will avail us of deeper existential concerns and rationalise social problems. Whilst newspaper headlines continue to overplay advances in genetics, follow-up studies never support initial claims or enjoy prominent reportage leaving only enduring promise. And the irony of searching for a magic pill to stop people from wanting the magic pill remains lost. As Herbert (Undated) identifies, a deep paradox is emerging from genetics, which belies the mechanistic vision it often portrays, 'The harder we work to demonstrate the power of hereditary, the harder it is to escape the potency of experience.' This is not to discount the valuable role genetics and neurology may yet play in our understanding of dependence. These are very new sciences and will continue to advance. But genes cannot be understood as both their own cause and effect. We simply cannot take the human out of human nature. And what makes us human is more than what lies beneath the skin.

Adapted from 'The Nature or Nurture Debate', *Addiction Today*. March 2002

# Chapter 5

# The Binds that Tie

*Such is not the course adopted by tyranny in democratic republics; there the body is left free, and the soul is enslaved. The master no longer says: 'You shall think as I do or you shall die'; but he says: 'You are free to think differently from me and to retain your life, your property, and all that you possess; but you are henceforth a stranger among your people.'*

Alexis de Tocqueville

In conversations with young problematic drug users, I was always stuck by a similar pattern. When we would discuss their past histories there were rarely the abuse issues that one so often expects. Nor did they ever report that they were simply compelled to use by their own bodies. There would often be the usual tensions that occur in growing up and family lives. But when I asked about how they saw their futures, they would always pause. They struggled to answer with any real clarity about how they saw their life course. It was as if they gazed not into the unknown, but a complete void. And similarly, if they had managed to get drug free, the reason for relapse offered was inevitably boredom. What struck me about their motivation to take drugs was not a biological imperative but personal meaning.

## Addicted to addiction?

It has long been recognised that hospital patients exposed to large doses of very pure opiates do not experience withdrawal or feel a deep compulsion to resume use post-treatment. Within street using populations withdrawal symptoms have no correlation to the amounts or duration of heroin used in street users. Novice users can have profound symptoms, experienced users very mild. The avoidance of withdrawal and cravings, so often cited as the biological reason that people continue to use drugs, does not explain that post-detoxification, people once again resume use. Numerous research studies into alcohol and drug consumption confirm that dependency is not even a steady state in itself, but fluctuates dramatically according to the individual's life circumstance (Edwards and Gross, 1976; Stimson and Oppenhiemer, 1982; Prochaska and DiClemente, 1982). With compulsivity correlating with negative reinforcers and limited access to enrichment, such as unemployment, unstable marriages, low income, prison incarceration and downward social drift or the unique problems in modern warfare (Bickel and DeGrandpre, 1995;

Robins et al., 1980). Furthermore, treatment outcomes themselves are not dependant on levels or frequency of consumption (Hser et al., 1998). Even supporters of the biological root of addiction observe, '. . . prognosis is much better in opiod addicts who are professionals, such as physicians and nurses, than in individuals with poor education and no legitimate job prospects, who are addicted to the same or even lesser amounts of opiods obtained on the street and financed by crime' (O'Brien and McCellen, 1996). Assessing medical functioning and social functioning both correlate in estimating the degree of problematic use (Vaillant, 1995), but the extent to which an individual experiences cultural separation is a more significant factor in the treatment outcome than their biology. As clients report in clinical practice, detoxification is easy: staying clean is the challenge.

Bandura, the architect of cognitive behavioural counselling approaches, once observed that the greatest indicator of failure is the expectation of failure. The 'once an addict always an addict' ethos of drug treatment is the most likely factor for turning a lapse into a relapse (Annis et al., 1996). In untreated groups, natural remission rates are far higher than in treatment remission groups (Robins, 1980). Walters (2000) review of remission studies suggested that between 4.3 and 56.4 per cent of users quit use without any treatment whatsoever. The mean average was 26.2 per cent over an average 5.3 years follow-up period. Those using alcohol experienced a 31.4 per cent remission rate, drug users experienced a 37.9 per cent remission rate with only 13.5 per cent of smokers entering into untreated remission. From these findings we can deduce that treatment outcomes are not linked to an abnormal appetite that cannot be assuaged by any means other than clinical interventions. Such experiences refute the biomedical depiction of the universally seductive power of the drug's action as the sole determining cause of compulsive use in humans and that addiction is a necessarily progressive illness.

## Content over construct

We must make a clear difference between two concepts which are not well defined but often used interchangeably. In the 1970s the World Health Organisation brought together a team of experts to define a conceptual framework for alcoholism, but the definition has been applied widely to all psychoactive substances. The definition, formulated by Edwards and Gross (1976), defined addiction as a 'clinical impression' of a dependence syndrome with a biological or psychological basis. Their criteria includes continued use regardless of the social context or mood state; use is a central priority in the individual's life; tolerance increases and the symptoms of withdrawal are present on cessation; individuals avoid withdrawal symptoms by continued use; there is self-awareness of a compulsion to use; and despite periods of abstinence, use is reinstated. Whilst 'dependence' has become the preferred name due to the negative connotations implicit in the word 'addict', there is a clinical difference between them. Dependence is defined by the presence of tolerance and withdrawal.

As such it can be considered a clinical syndrome, and largely a medical issue. Addiction, however, describes impairment in social functioning, where the drug is a central focus of the user. It is a preoccupation with one source of satisfaction that erodes all other relationships, priorities or concerns; be they social, physical, economical or cultural. As such it invokes inevitable social, cultural and economic forces which enhance or impede access to substances. Along with cultural and legal strictures which divide the socially acceptable behaviours from the socially repugnant ones. For example within Western culture, individuals may be dependant on nicotine, but the wide access, relatively cheap cost, legal status and social acceptance means that these individuals' lives are not disrupted by their use as they are for a drug like heroin. Addiction is not simply the biological action of the drug, but the cultural context in which the drug is taken.

As we have seen, humans cannot be understood as primarily biological beings. Culture overrules our biology at every step. We must eat but people observe Ramadan or go on hunger strike because it is a more meaningful way of life. We have sexual drives but every culture observes incest taboos because it is a more meaningful way of life. We are supposed to live long enough to pass on genetics to our children, but millions of young men have laid down their lives in war because it is a more meaningful way of life. In the natural world it would make no biological sense for a creature to endlessly pursue dried wood pulp with inky stains upon it which is not even edible. But money drives the cultural world we inhabit. If we consider the human operations that are purely biological such as sex, eating, excretion and dying, three are completely hidden from the public gaze, whilst the fourth, eating, has been ritualised to the point that practically disguises its function. We are not at ease with our biological realities, and comfort ourselves in our cultural constructions.

Likewise, pharmacological treatments may mimic or impede the interactions of drugs at a neurological level but they cannot address the experience which transcends it. For example, in the 1960s, the policy of allowing British doctors to prescribe drugs of choice to addicts attracted international attention. It inspired a sizeable population of heroin-dependent Canadians to migrate to Britain. Although they were indeed prescribed drugs of choice once they had settled here, many returned to Canada shortly afterwards because they missed their previous lifestyle (Durlacher, 2000). Similarly, studies exploring heroin use amongst American GIs in Vietnam revealed that 50 per cent were addicted to heroin. But only 14 per cent of this group continued to use it after undergoing the profound environmental shift of returning to the United States. Many of those GIs who did continue to use heroin used it recreationally, without developing the extreme range of behaviours we normally ascribe to heroin use (Robins et al., 1980). Those whose use remained problematic upon return were prey to a plethora of social problems before going to the war. This variance cannot be attributed to the effects of the traumas of war on human psychology itself, as very few troops actually saw active combat (see Dean,

1997). Boredom was the greatest enemy separated from the routines, relationships and concerns of their every day 'home' lives.

Within street addicted populations, satisfying a biological need for drugs is not enough when it does not satisfy the need for a purposeful life that surrounds it, no matter how meagre. Isadore Chien et al. (1964), who spent years studying inner city heroin users, came to suggest that people do not become attached to the drug but to the 'addict' lifestyle. Lifestyles which offered otherwise disenfranchised individuals a meaningful structure and purpose to their lives, having to get up, 'score', acquire money, evade detection and receive payment for labour invested in illicit substances. All associations revolve around the drug, ethics are determined by the natural justice that comes from living beyond the influence of law, and behaviours are normalised and permissible within this context. Chien et al. stated that these young people appeared to be 'educated in their own incompetence from the day they were born'. As such they characterised chronic use as a 'career' for those outside of mainstream society. It can be understood as the total immersion in a shadow society where the only meaning and satisfaction available is drug induced.

Those that maintain wider webs of relationships and commitments outside their use, considered recreational users, may be dependant. But they are not experiencing the problems of exclusion and isolation of those addicted. One of the central problems in drug treatment is that we have mistaken medical treatments for dependence, as the solution to addiction. In practice you see little progress for addicted individuals on pharmacology interventions because we cannot prescribe a drug which heals family breakdown, cures unemployment, revises self-confidences, inures self-expectations or replicates the skills for life. The temperance heritage of addiction as an event located *within* the individual has distracted us from addiction as an event *between* the individual and the demands of their environment. This is why addiction did not exist prior to the 18th century. As it is only when the water-mark of cultural demands are raised, that those without the resources or who are impeded, become jettisoned from social structures.

## A Foucaultian fallacy

After two hundred years of domination, the temperance ideological belief systems are finally being questioned. There is an emergence of new thinking that understands addiction not as a private event located in an individual's biology or psychology, but as the product of an individual's interaction with the cultural forces that enmesh them. But the culturalisation of addiction is not without irony. As cultural and literary theorist Terry Eagleton (2000) warns, culturalism may be as deterministic as the biological sciences. Alternatively, under the sway of post-Foucault historical critiques of social structures which give pre-eminence to all human life as purely cultural, many cultural thinkers have come to regard treatment for addiction as merely social control: drug use is not problematic but the political-cultural context is. It is vicariously inferred that, if we stop interfering in people's behaviour, then a 'natural' regulatory mechanism will come into play that will immunise them from drug problems. Dole (1986) rightly comments that social improvement as the only means to address addiction is utopian in light of any political system's failure to truly address poverty and deprivation. But there is a deeper fallacy. If we accept addiction is a cultural problem, not a biological one, it does not follow that they are not 'really' problematic as is sometimes assumed to be implicit in such statements. The converse is actually true. Addiction would be eminently easier to treat if it was a biological concern that could be erased with a medical treatment.

Both biological and cultural fundamentalism overrules personal meaning (Jencks, 2001). Culture is the menu but not the course. Whilst the over-arching architecture of culture has become increasingly globalised, it has fragmented into a myriad of sub-cultures through which individuals are both born, but also seek, expressions that harmonise with their identity. Advertising and marketing companies have been far more successful in understanding the idiosyncratic hopes and fears of these sub-groups than the grand theories of therapy (Solomon et al., 1999). I would suggest that the difference between these sub-cultures is only one of personal ethics. All our life courses pass through dominant cultural structures such as family, school, work and relationships. Whilst they run parallel, it is the personal ethics we subscribe to and our economic circumstances that streamline us into different cultural strata.

Within this, (sub)cultures have used and will always use drugs as a totemistic commodity that is meaningful to them (Lury, 1996). Totemistic objects are the focal point around which individuals form collective group identities as a symbolic expression of their ethics. Hence the value of these objects does not lie in their economic worth but in the meaning these groups ascribe to them. For those on the fringe of society, drugs become more than chemical duty free. They become an expression of ethics, where like-minded individuals are drawn to the same totemistic object, forming groups of identity with similar values.

The Research Business International commissioned the very first consumer report on the activities of cannabis smokers on behalf of high street retailers in lieu of possible changes in consumption from decriminalisation (Summerskill, 2003). This research is interesting because very clear common ethical patterns emerged. They found cannabis smokers were 'Young people between the age of 15-30 and were very trend conscious and aspirational.' They shunned 'corporate' businesses such as McDonalds and Starbucks. If they went for a night out, they avoided venues associated with heavy drinking. The illegality of their use led to the creation of a six billion pound economy in home entertainment. Here these social networks smoke cannabis along with other activities such as playing computer games, watching videos, listening to music and eating takeaway food in group settings. What we see here is the evolution of distinct social behaviour clustered around the 'totem' of cannabis. The drug is not just a reason for these groups to meet but allows for a certain kind of social interaction with like-minded others. Each drug sub-culture has its parallel expressions of ethics and permissible behaviours. Heavy drug use can be seen as an *habitués*, a certain way of life. It is not about biology but the lifestyle framework that the user surrounds themself with. And the legal and social sanctions against illegal drugs can be as corrosive as individual desires and may ultimately exclude people from society, deepening the individual's enmeshment in these sub-cultures. As mounting losses accumulate, the only positive or affirming experience they have access to is the drug, amplifying its significance.

There is evidence that this applies to all drug using groups who evolve their own normative fallacy of behaviours (Grund, 1993). Whereby users mistake the in-group norms for the way of living, amending and making permissible, new behaviours and ethics. Many of these values may be in contradiction to perceived social norms. This has been to the extent whereby even non-users may affiliate and share in the behaviours of problematic users in order to belong. For example, Gay et al. (1973) charted the rise in presentation to methadone treatment services of non-addicted individuals in the Haight-Ashbury district of San Francisco. These 'pseudo junkies' outwardly presented as heroin addicts in all but one critical area. They tested negative for opiates. But they did appear drawn to the illegitimate lifestyle and values of the 'junkie' themselves. Within this there is no reason to assume every excluded community of drug users will be identical as they formulate their own values and expectancies. Indeed the regional variance in drug use, administration and slang, underscore that the informal web of drug using relationships disseminate their own evolved norms and values, interpreted from the wider cultural perspective of use.

The central problem for addiction treatment is once an individual is subsumed in these norms, and embedded in this web of relationships, it is difficult to address specific behaviours which are otherwise normalised by these groups. It is telling that prison sentencing as punishment evolved in reaction to social deviancy. The Inquisition recognised that martyrdom of individuals did little to stop the spread of heresy, only by disrupting the web of associations within groups sharing similar values could they halt the dissemination of radical ideas and new norms. I am not recommending this as the action to address addiction. Drug use in itself does not make an individual dangerous, nor necessitate punishment. Rather I wish to underline addiction is more than the individual, it is locked into a web of relationships and contextual factors. And addiction treatment should not limit itself to being a discrete cure of the individual self. For whilst the individual remains secured in certain relationships and excluded from others, drug use will remain salient, regardless of their biological status. As Robins (1993) concluded in the study of cessation of use in the returning Vietnam war vets, 'As I look back at the Vietnam heroin experience, I conclude the soldiers had no special readiness to use narcotics or to recover from addiction to them. Their remarkable rate of use was a response to the market conditions – both the high availability of opiates and the lack of alternative recreational substances, to the absence of disapproving friends and relatives, and to the fact that serving in Vietnam was not seen as their real life career. *Their readiness to recover from addiction did not differ from that of other users'* (my emphasis).

## Conclusion

Addiction emerges and is sustained in the (sub)cultural context. Biology's role is much overplayed in light of these contexts, augmented by a cultural view of individualism, where human nature is confined to the limits of their biological or psychological operation. But as we progress through the cultural institutions of life, the contexts of behaviour change, and with them our values, meaning and self-identity. We are the expression of our ethics and we are wrapped in networks which sustain them. And as these networks change, then so do we. If we take a longitudinal perspective, rather than the client's presenting moment, we see the fluxes in consumption unravel and recede. These findings may do much to illuminate this interaction and define the context for treatment.

Based on 'Barriers to Treatment', A conference organised by young drug users, Gloucester, 11th June 2002

# Chapter 6

# Natural Born Quitters

*Choose Life. Choose a job. Choose a career. Choose a family. Choose a big fucking television, choose washing machines, cars, compact disc players and electrical tin openers. Choose good health, low cholesterol and dental insurance. Choose fixed interest mortgage repayments. Choose a starter home. Choose your friends. Choose leisure wear and matching luggage. Choose a three piece suite on hire purchase in a range of fucking fabrics. Choose DIY and wondering who the fuck you are on a Sunday morning. Choose sitting on that couch watching mind numbing, spirit crushing games shows, stuffing fucking junk food into your mouth. Choose rotting away at the end of it all, pishing (Scotish vernacular) your last in a miserable home, nothing more than an embarrassment to the selfish fucked up brats you spawned to replace yourself. Choose your future. Choose Life. But why would I want to do a thing like that?'*

Irvine Welsh

Drug prevention, education and treatment remain a social priority; yet all too often pragmatic responses have been drowned out by a moral imperative to halt, rather than address these abiding human concerns. Our efforts have been well intentioned but have missed key issues in development and change processes, hampering the effectiveness of both informing and helping. This has limited our thinking to a narrow set of concerns that focuses our attention almost exclusively on the biology of drug use and on the most problematic experiences. And to mistake these extremes as the totality of the drug using experience renders our authority wholly naive in those at risk at either end of the using continuum. It is important to widen our focus by exploring drug use in its development and remission, where problematic use ceases without recourse to treatment. This is not to dismiss our roles but to illuminate key factors that we must grasp if we are to be more effective in education and treatment.

## Lost causes

Every academic discipline has attempted to reduce human development to the most basic unit. Psychology, sociology, social psychology and biology have all tried to monopolise human development in their own way. It is not surprising that individually these disciplines have failed to identify any single causal mechanism for addiction which they can call their own. The distinct nature of these disciplines in themselves is a bureaucratic divide which cannot encompass the full human experience. Reductionism is a cultural product not a reality. In spite of this, each discipline has evolved ever more complex models which can be as imponderable as the very phenomena they hope to simplify. As such, reductionism remains a fallacy, as models become not simplistic but delve ever deeper in their own concerns.

We have already seen that one major obstacle is our own cultural perspective of democratic-liberalism places great emphasis on individualism. This bias has created a very 'autistic' vision of human nature. When we observe human development, we focus on the individual mind or their biology. But the context in which this individual operates is also vital. Human beings only make sense in a context. We exist as a physical entity and a psychological one. For development to occur the young person needs their biological growth and self-awareness. But they are also drawing resources from the wider social framework. We have internal direction but we also are shaped by the patterns of family that nurture us through the most vulnerable years. Outside peers have a huge impact on our behaviour, as they support risk taking and greater autonomy away from the family. Against this backdrop the legal, political and economic circumstance pervades and structures our lives. Schools, the law, opportunity for employment, social mores of sex, love and courtship all set the perimeters and expectations of our life.

Within this we must recognise that we are more than our biology. We do not form relationships with any people, we do not buy any clothes, we do not drive any car, live in any district or do any job. We chose from the overarching menu of our culture and within the prescribed range of choice we find the trappings to express ethics and forge identities which are meaningful to us. Poverty and exclusion in a materialistic culture precludes people from forming this richer and extended version of self. Whilst the trapping of material excess may condemn the wealthy to the indolent lives which lack any deeper purpose. As Bourdieu (Robbins, 2000) observes, within these social strata runs a cultural war of taste. We mistake *our* ways of living as *the* way of living. As such, we cannot be seen as a neat little identity, divorced from this web of relationships. The world we are embedded in is as important as the individual who is embedded. Throughout our lives we reside in contexts and environments that we may have little or no control over when we are young, and then are culturally tasked with creating for ourselves when an adult.

## Risk factors

When reviewing the risk factors for the development of addiction we see they are spread across the key domains of the individual, family, social and cultural. The community a child is born into intensifies the risk of problematic drug use. It includes social acceptance of use and sets the legally permissible age for alcohol consumption. At a more immediate level, increased availability of drugs in the area, low cost of the drugs themselves and lack of alternative opportunities conspire to make use ever more desirable and obtainable. Poverty and deprivation are also major factors, especially in urban areas where there is a high turnover in residents, little community attachment and where the visible effects of urban blight smother a sense of hope.

Within the family structure, high use by parents or siblings, poor modelling of behaviour and emotional instability in the father have been identified as contributory factors. Along with little parental control, marital or family discord in low achievement, low expectation family groups. Current peer use is a major predictor of future use in young people residing within the normative fallacy of behaviour. But this may be especially the case in antisocial groups with little boundaries and self-regulation. Problematic use also shows high correlation with truancy, failure at school, poor educational achievement (Sullivan and Farrell, 2002). Within the individual, research suggests that they may have vulnerability factors, either biologically or psychologically. And for their long term prognosis, age of onset remains very important in predicting the frequency and range of future drug use (Dadds and McAloon, 2001).

As such no single site for addiction will be discovered within the individual or in the environment, as it exists as a breakdown *between* these domains. It is disappointing that more research is not spent in understanding how these different domains interact with each other. Because it is these interactions, so often characterised by disruptions in a person's life that are sources of maladaptive behaviours. Furthermore, the more domains in which these problems occur, the deeper the problems are ingrained. For example, a young person's drug use that occurs exclusively amongst peers is far easier to address than an individual whose drug use occurs with peers, in isolation, in family and in school. As a result, research demonstrates that treatments across all domains of family, schools as well as the individual, produce far greater outcomes than those that occur solely in the individual domain.

## Time goes by

We cannot truly understand drug use in cross section. Young people are growing fast physically, emotionally, socially and cognitively. We must map this growth and observe where drug use evolves and dissipates within this development. Our development can be characterised by key stages. These stages are defined by our culture. As such, culture is not some distant set of biases which influences our thinking in some way. These cultural values have a physical manifestation in the laws, institutions and demarcations on acceptable relationships and permissible behaviours which shape our lives. For example, we have created the institution of school because as adults we must operate in a market place where we will come to buy and sell specialist knowledge. School is the cultural preparation for a very specific type of adult life. As Lasch (1991) commented, this demands we raise our children to manage a dire tension of modern life, to be ruthless competitors but with a smile to facilitate the negotiations of the market place. Agricultural societies need to give their children agricultural toys, warrior societies warrior toys. Indeed it would be a harsh culture that did not prepare its children for the demands that will await them.

Cultural institutions bind us to aggregated norms of the context. It sets the parameters for the standard distribution curve of behaviour. For example, in the work place you do not do the work 'your way', but the 'organisational way'. Deviation from the mean is not simply mathematical, we are punished for acting outside the acceptable perimeters in life, work and our relationships. Whilst cultural institutions may be pervasive and monumental; this is not to suggest they are immutable. Cultural norms shift and change through formal or informal processes. From the rise of computing and Nazism, to the decline of smoking nicotine and watching cricket matches, meanings and preferences are amended and re-constituted all the time in both evolutionary and revolutionary cultural shifts.

Western culture forces us through social structures that define our activities, behaviour and the way we make sense of the world (Kegan, 1982). What we see in Western culture is that our first phase of embeddedness is in the mother, until the age of two when we become embedded in the family. But we must ready our children to take up specialised roles in becoming consumers and producers in a capitalist economy. So, at five we are excluded from the parental bed and even the home as we are embedded in school life with our peers. A mother cries on the child's first day at school as she knows she surrenders her ward to the world. Here we receive our formal education, but also an informal one of socialisation. Children for the most part socialise each other, through the rough justice of the playground and the glowing prize of acceptance and popularity (Harris, 1999). On leaving school, we join a sub-culture of people who share our values. We may join the army, go to university, head off travelling or even take up residence in a squat or shared house. Whilst the ethics of these choices vary, they have the same function in bridging us out of the family home. Until at last we join the institutional life, marriage, our own families, mortgages and careers. When all our parents' reactionary platitudes, once derided as so outmoded, suddenly make a great deal of sense. Embedded in these niches, we not only behave differently, but our values and means of making sense of the world are different. This is because different demands and responsibilities are placed upon us, and different expectations are to be fulfilled within each stage of the life course. And the rampant expression of the unfettered self is not one of them.

## Between the lines

Drug use arises between the adolescent peer and the institutional world. This is an important transition where we move from the embeddedness of others (parents, school, peers), to having to create our own embeddedness (jobs, partners, families). Defining this future life course places immense and obvious stresses on the individual. In Western culture, we are allowed a moratorium to find ourselves. The late teens through to the mid-twenties is a time when we can sample different modes of adult life and flirt with creating our 'world'. It is not until the age of 25 (approximately) that we feel pressured to settle (Robbins and Wilner, 2001). A fact played on mercilessly by advertisers. If we do not attain the life we desire for ourselves or feel desperately off track, the age 30 crisis can precipitate a major re-evaluation of our priorities (Levinson, 1986; Marcia, 1987; Whitbourne et al., 1992). It is at this age we realise a balance has shifted. We may have more history than destiny. The passing of years makes us focus on what is important to us, what we want to do with our lives and who we want to do it with. The first intimation of mortality drives us to express ethics that are important to us demanding radical change if necessary.

The interim period between adolescence and adulthood is the highest risk period for problematic drug use (Kandel, 1995). But since the early 1960s it had been observed that people appeared to age out of opiate use by the ages of 35–40 (Stall and Biernaki, 1986). Though there is evidence to suggest that due to racism, which tends to exclude people from the social institutions of life at a younger age, exclusion occurs sooner and remains protracted for longer as people are denied re-entry (Kandel, 1995). Alcoholism tends to occur in the early 30s–60s (Vaillant, 1995). Here it seems to be associated with the destruction of the institutional adult life that people have created for themselves, who feel the loss cannot be replaced. Job loss, divorce, the increasing pressure of family life in small nuclear units and unemployment can all contribute to the pressures of transition at this time of life. At the point of separation, men's use reverts to that of their single peers whilst women's use of alcohol can go off the scale under the burden of child rearing and poverty. An early onset of alcoholism can occur and tends to be more entrenched to treat. In this respect they may share common developmental issues with the younger drug user.

Risk factors seem to increase for individuals that can be described as highly externalised (the under-parented) and the internalised (the over-parented). These groups grow up in family units of two extremes. The externalised family tends to be permissive and exert little control over the development of the young person, model poor behaviour around high consumption and exert little influence on the peer groups that the offspring subscribe too. Internals tend to be raised by abstinent, fretful parents who may overprotect their offspring from risk and responsibility, censure peer contact and thus disconnect their children from the socialisation process (Dadds and McAloon, 2001). Children forced into care taking roles also face similar over enmeshment in the family life. It is these over and under attachments that allow drift from the cultural institutions of life to occur. And ensuing separation from these contexts may deepen the problems people experience.

## Too much and too little

In the under-parented group, drug use tends to occur sooner, where they become increasingly detached from the cultural institutions in deference to the all important peer group. Positive expectations of use can soon erode support structures in their lives such as school and family. In our over-parented group, the lack of socialisation limits pre-exposure to intoxication and appears to delay their involvement in drugs. But at the same time, it denies them the opportunity to develop self-regulatory behaviour around intoxication too. Once separation from the family does occur it results in a bout of youthful consumption that rises dramatically. Those feeling socially awkward can find themselves attracted to and embedded in drug using sub-groups who are more accepting of social maladaption than other groups.

What is interesting is that in both high and low consuming young people, all move towards a cultural average of alcohol consumption post-adolescence. They retain their rank order, but move towards the average, with young people who do not consume alcohol increasing intake whilst high consumers decrease intake (Pape and Hammer, 1996). This is with one caveat. The higher and more chaotic the drug use, the greater likelihood of total abstinence (Erikson and Hadaway, 1989). But generally speaking, total abstinence has a negative impact on young people in making them feel culturally deviant in other ways (see Chapter 7, The Apprenticeship for Life).

Initially drug use may serve as a central reference point for the peer group. It serves as a group totem bringing together like-minded others. But if people funnel their attention into this sole pursuit, which is normalised in family, peer and community, with little competing reinforcing behaviours, the corrosive effects soon mount. This is especially true for the 'confident incompetent', whose expectation of self-control far exceeds their actual ability (Bandura, 1997). The incremental exclusion into the shadow society of drug use serves to widen their separation from the mainstream. As this occurs individuals may find themselves under increasing psychological, family, health or criminal justice pressures. The meaning of use can change, becoming the only source of relief from increased tensions and alienation. Until eventually drugs become both the coping strategy and source of increasing turbulence. As such, the risk of developing drug and alcohol problems appears stratified, as risk varies with every escalation in use. The relentless pursuit of drugs in a shadow society of using peers occupies these young people's time. Time others are rehearsing and developing within the demands of cultural frameworks, preparing them for adult life. Addiction thus does not merely disconnect but inures developmental delay in the user, whose singular preoccupation is leaving them ever more unrehearsed for the increasingly complex demands of adult life. Drugs' capacity as a positive reinforcer is magnified against this backdrop of increasing social disconnection and drift.

Dramatic economic changes have meant that the predicted life route for many in these groups is no longer there. Semi-skilled labour markets have collapsed leaving many individuals and entire communities marooned from the expected life journeys to adulthood, developing a sense of identity and worth through employment and providing themselves with the financial means to acquire other sources of satisfaction. The adult life that many expect for themselves has disappeared in a rapidly changing marketplace. Drugs can provide the only form of purposeful activity and the only source of satisfaction to those culturally stranded. These swift changes in the labour market have primarily influenced male roles as bread winners. Women's role as carers has changed to a lesser degree. If anything one might suggest it has intensified this role in these social strata as they take care of males dislocated from their former sources of worth and satisfaction.

## The shadow society

Drug addiction can be seen as a form of embeddedness in a shadow sub-culture for those unable to construct a meaningful life within the cultural milieu. We must recognise that once embedded in these problematic groups, separated from the cultural map and becoming increasingly developmentally adrift, the problematic user has greater problems than merely overcoming the 'wants' of their biology. Their identity, their meaning and purpose in life and the force that connects them to other people is the drug. Change does not merely imply stopping use, but redefining one's entire life. It is not just about escaping addiction but escaping the context that makes addiction meaningful and catching up with the demands of an institutional life that they may have little or no prior experience of. We would not expect a 14 year-old to competently meet the demands of a 35 year-old. They have neither the skills, the experience or cognitive capacity to do so. But we expect it of the newly drug free individual. And when they fail we call it the disease.

Once deeply embedded in the shadow society, divorced from the institutions of life, and under increasing external pressures, this lifestyle becomes increasingly untenable to sustain. Problems with health, mental health, criminal justice, family separation, child rearing, self-loathing exceed a drug's capacity to sedate. Alternatively individuals who seek deep relief from life in isolation for fear of exposure, still disconnect from others. Social sanctions on consumption are negated, time is spent alone deepening alienation until other aspects of their life are threatened. Crisis points figure highly in non-treatment seekers' accounts of what motivates them to change (Miller, 1998; Klingemann, 1991; Stall and Biernacki, 1986; Burman, 1997). This may be the shame of current behaviour or an existential guilt that the individual is not reaching their potential (Van Kalmthout, 1991). It can be triggered by mundane events or through hitting 'rock bottom'. Hitting rock bottom is the realisation that one now dwells in a personal hell, one which no chemical consumption has the potency to subdue. This realisation can be sparked through quiet reflection when the environmental distractions of the addictive life is turned down, to a profound spiritual reawakening (Miller and C'de Baca, 1994; C'de Baca and Wilbourne, 2004). Whilst these events can happen in the natural course of use, and indeed happen to non-users, some research suggests that they may be initiated by some previous low dose treatment intervention (Cunningham, 2000). What we see here is that addiction provides not only meaning and purpose to the user's life, but the critical factor in change is again deeply entwined in a breakdown in meaning and the re-evaluation of self-identity. Drug use changes as it becomes increasingly incompatible with an emergent sense of oneself.

## Coming up

Certainly, cessation of use occurs as individuals prepare to enter into institutional life. When interviewed, natural remitters report that jobs, partners, families, and non-using peer groups soon crowd out use once the individual moves towards the labour market (Erikson and Hadaway, 1989; Stall and Biernacki, 1986). We see the individual shift in cultures of identity into ones that feel more meaningful to them, and begin to reach their potential. Certainly, in the institutional phase of our lives, couples tend to socialise with couples, those with children hang out with those with children, and those at work socialise within their workforce. Such new affiliations strangle out the monopoly of drug using peers (Labouvie, 1996).

Research into natural remission in untreated groups mirrors this very process. It highlights three necessary conditions: separation from certain sub-cultures; emergence of a new identity with an incumbent ethics; and establishment within a new sub-culture that supports these ethics (Stall and Biernacki, 1986; Klingemann, 1992). Anyone who has faced a life-changing choice, such as a career shift, divorce or emigration, will understand the magnitude of such a reappraisal. Some problematic drug users do not feel ready for such far-reaching change despite the onset of crises and difficulties. They may instead choose to improve the quality of life within their problematic sub-culture. They will opt for 'light therapy', which will reduce the level of suffering within this culture of identity. Methadone, harm reduction and needle exchanges reduce the negative forces that mount upon them and their use. Confusion arises when these light therapies are relied upon to produce deeper gains. Substitute pharmacology such as methadone can enable separation from drug-using networks, which can be an important first step, but will not provide the means for deeper re-engagement to occur. But in clinical practice methadone efficacy is reduced because individuals remain embedded in using relationships. Light therapy outcomes should therefore be measured according to how successfully they help reduce negative forces in clients' lives, such as reducing offending, family disruption, and health problems.

For those who feel ready to change, we see a 'deep therapy' process of rebuilding one's life. This involves skills, relationship building, family connection, overcoming stigma and fusing all the links that bring us back to the cultural map. Such an undertaking is massive. It is not always achieved at the first attempt. What these programmes do achieve is significantly reducing use with every treatment episode, and there is strong evidence to suggest treatment speeds up this process of reintegration. In this way drug use is curtailed in stages (Prochaska et al., 1994; Hser et al., 1998). The exact same process occurs in natural remitters.

The confusion of these two orders of treatment is personified in the trend to coerce drug users into treatment programmes under the government initiatives to reduce offending. In clinical settings there was a great deal of resistance to accepting offenders on programmes, particularly in residential settings, across the 1980s. A common wisdom prevailed that they were unmotivated, unengaged and seeking a softer option than prison. However, since large sums of government funding has become available, drug services quickly entered into a Faustian pact with criminal justice services, in what could be essentially considered as a takeover bid. In their defence, drug services and government were quick to cite research that suggested that there was no clinical difference in outcome between voluntary and involuntary clients. A paper universally cited in support was Anglin et al. (1989). However, this research is a comparison of voluntary and involuntary opiate users on *long term methadone maintenance* prescriptions. The high demand for this 'light' therapy within this client group is not comparable with the expectation that coerced clients will make 'deep' change just as easily. Indeed, research on the effectiveness of Drug Testing and Treatment Orders, placing a mandatory requirement on drug using offenders to enter into treatment, has highlighted this. Launched nationally before the pilots were completed, each county can prescribe its own requirements. The Gloucestershire pilot's deep therapy demanded total abstinence within weeks of entry on the programme and as a result over 60 per cent of the orders were revoked, principally for non-attendance. Whereas in Liverpool, only 'light therapy' demands were made and only 28 per cent of orders were revoked (Ashton, 2001). Whilst the pilot did identify some reductions in use and crime, it relied heavily on the verbal reports of these coerced clients which did not correlate well with urine samples.

The conflict between light and deep therapy places drug services in a double bind. Light therapies may improve the quality of people's suffering within their existing relationship but this will negate anxiety and concerns which research demonstrates is a vital component of deep change. Alternatively it would be inhumane to retract these interventions in the face of so much suffering. Hence many active users desperately seek methadone, whilst many ex-users state that methadone robbed them of many years of their life by sustaining them in using networks. I do not advocate one form of treatment over the other, and there is no simple resolution to this paradox of treatment. But first and foremost it is important to recognise that this contradiction is at the very heart of drug work.

Culturally we have come to shun the crises moment. We wish to sedate it through pharmacology or mollify it through counselling interventions. What we miss in doing so is the therapeutic value of crises. The breakdown in meaning may serve as an opportunity to evolve into new identities and allow the emergence of new values. If we consider our own lives, it was these moments of crises that redefined us and provided a powerful impetus for growth and change. And problematic users are no different.

## Conclusion

Those who use drugs recreationally remain in contact with their cultural journey (the vast majority in fact). They may be tipped into problematic use but on the whole lead lives which are enriched with many sources of satisfaction and purposeful activity which stop drug use and drug using peers dominating. Addiction is deeply entwined in the life course. Many problematic consumers of substances can and do change without recourse to treatment, either psychological or pharmacological. What we see in this characterisation is that cultural separation for the problematic user is deeply apparent. If we are to address this we must recognise that treatment cannot be *supra-cultural* in providing this group with something beyond the ken of the rest of us. The lessons we might learn are how to configure treatment to enhance and speed up this process. As such, treatment must span all domains of the individual life. People need to reconnect with their cultural map and need the skills deficits that have resulted from their development delay to be redressed. The narrowness of our concerns does not adequately address the deficits and ruptures across the human experience and so we limit our gains and sustain our relapse rates accordingly. For too long we have ascribed individual's failures as a symptom of their disease. As workers in the field, we must confront the possibility that failure may also be a symptom of the treatment. What this demands is a better understanding of how people actually change. And this is the area we shall explore next.

Based on a presentation to the Stakeholders Conference in support of On the Level, Somerset, 7th February 2003

# Chapter 7

# The Apprenticeship for Life

*All things are changing; and we are changing with them.*

Nicholas Borbonius (Attributed)

Drugs are portrayed as the source of all social evils, from individual dereliction to crime, promiscuity and family breakdown, even to the very erosion of society itself. As early as 1922, social demons of the drug menace entered the popular imagination, with the publication of the bestselling book on drugs, *The Black Candle* (Murphy, 1922). Its depiction of merciless dealers at the school gates, crazed black rapists high on coke and virginal teenage girls lured into vice and death for their want of cannabis still resonates today. The crusade to save young people from this pharmacological destitution has led to the loss of both logic and good sense. We rarely ask what drug use means to young people, or what is it that actually causes them problems.

## What are we doing?

Whilst some UK research has estimated drug use amongst young people is as high as 67 per cent (Williamson, 1997) the government's own figures indicate that amongst 11–15 year-olds, 12 per cent used drugs in the last month and 20 per cent had done so in the last year (Department of Health, 2002). Drug use peaks between 14 and 25, by which time the vast majority of users will have stopped using without recourse to treatment (Parker et al., 1998). Measuring drug use is difficult, as desire for 'street credibility' leads some young people to increase estimates of their usage, while others, for fear of the consequences of disclosure, reduce it. Published surveys confuse the words 'use' with 'abuse', creating a more dramatic connotation, itself magnified by a failure to indicate which drugs are being used and at what frequency. In fact, most young people's experience of drugs is confined to cannabis and alcohol (Department of Health, 2002b).

There is no universal criterion for when use is a 'problem'. One could be classed as an addict in one country and be cured simply by crossing the border. As one epidemiologist observed, the futility of trying to assess the degree of problematic consumption should make any researcher 'leave the field before his reputation was hopelessly tarnished' (cf. Moore and Saunders, 1991).

All of these issues are compounded by the media's packaging of human tragedy. Leah Betts is a household name in a way that thousands of young people who have died through more common non-drug related misadventures are not. We forget that the media is drawn to the novel, and not the everyday. What we *can* discern is that a great number of young people will try drugs, and emerge unscathed from this experience. But is our desire to intervene helping or harming this process?

## Drug promotion programmes

A panoply of drug prevention initiatives has attempted to address drug use in young people. Primarily these offer very simplistic information on the major illicit drugs and their 'effects'. But as we have seen, the idea that specific drugs have fixed and predictable effects which do not vary from person to person is extremely widespread but remains a fallacy (Gossop, 1993). These programmes operate on the unfounded assumptions that knowledge changes behaviours, shock tactics prevent experimentation and that young people's use is fuelled by low self-esteem and an inability to resist their peers. It is a vision in which young people's drug use is an essentially moronic pursuit which compensates for self-loathing and the incapacity to resist the influence of equally debilitated friends. Inevitably the outcomes of these programmes are non-existent at best (Moore and Saunders, 1991). Reviewing their effectiveness, eminent professor of psychology Albert Bandura (1997) summarised, 'Programmes that merely convey information about addictive substances increase knowledge but achieve little else. Those that focus on building self-esteem and self-awareness and clarify feelings and values achieve little, if anything.'

## Nothing is better than anything

Despite such findings, the American billion dollar national programme 'Project DARE' is being exported across the world and attempts to do more of the same. An elaboration on the ridiculous 'Just Say No' campaigns, it still teaches kids the risks of drugs and to just say no but also to 'walk away'. Research has found it to be wholly ineffective and some American states have dropped the programme (DARE, 2000). DARE's director, Glen Lavant, responded to research findings with the mantra of drug preventionists the world over – 'Anything is better than nothing'. Such a stance removes all quality control and, effectively, allows anyone into our schools to say anything about drugs with no regard for its consequences. As leading addiction expert Stanton Peele (1995a) observes, this has led to murderers, rapists and petty criminals becoming role models, going into schools teaching young people how they screwed up. Those who have successfully avoided these problems are not invited because they are not seen as 'expert'.

In the 1970s, maverick thinkers such as Norman Zinberg (1984) observed that drugs prevention was actually encouraging use through stimulation of young people's curiosity. Follow-up research has borne this out. Prevention programmes normalise drug use, send the message that everyone else is taking them, romanticise risk taking factors through war stories of ex-users and promote the expectancy of loss of control. At the same time, the factual information given is so transparently biased that most young people reject it out of hand, reducing trust in engaging in any meaningful dialogue with adults (McFadyean, 1997). Certainly we are too apt at informing young people about the things that they should not do. But if we were to choose a diet for ourselves, would we choose one that offered us coloured brochures of all the rich puddings we could not eat, or the one that showed us the satisfying alternatives?

Drug prevention can be likened to the efforts of medieval monks, travelling from village to village warning of the plague whilst spreading it. It is of special note that Life Skills Training, the only prevention programme to demonstrate consistently effective outcomes (discussed later), works by challenging these very 'normative fallacies' propagated by other approaches (Stothard and Ashton, 2000).

## The doughnut effect

Treatment for the minority of young people who do have problems is worse. One government report highlighted that only a third of local authorities were strategically addressing young drug users' needs; another third did so poorly, whilst the rest paid it no attention at all (Social Services Inspectorate, 1997). In a national mapping exercise of young people's services, only 25 agencies were found to be operating within the government's guidelines and three-quarters of them had one youth worker or none at all (Drugscope, 1999). Gains have been made by increasing provision, but emerging government money is being ploughed into statutory services such as youth offending teams, child and adolescent mental health and social services departments. This creates a doughnut ring of services that only provide interventions to those at the most chaotic end of their usage, with no early interventions intercepting them en route.

Government has decreed that all treatment services for young people must be youth specific, reflecting the intrinsic differences between young people and adults. However, this is occurring in a knowledge void. What usually passes for youth specific often amounts to nothing more than labelling problematic behaviours or pathologising young people as deviant, dressed up in buzz diagnoses such as attention deficit hyperactivity disorder or autistic spectrum. Most of these 'youth specific' programmes are designed in accordance with adult ideals and impose total abstinence upon their wards, regardless of young people's own wishes or readiness to change. Whilst guidelines exist, they are recommendations only, and do not provide a framework within which to work with young people (SCODA/CLC, 1999). Only with a deeper understanding of adolescent development can we orient ourselves towards their needs and not our own.

## Same picture, different frame

Whilst many models of adolescent development abound (see McIlveen and Gross, 1997; Sugarman, 2000), I owe much to educational psychologist Robert Kegan (1982) and his hugely important but little known text, *The Evolving Self*. Kegan's model of development suggests that, as we mature, the way we make sense of the world changes. This is because we occupy different cultural niches and institutions which place specific and increasingly sophisticated demands upon us. These stratified cultural demands challenge our thinking, create new expectations and shift increasing responsibility on the individual at a challenging, but not formidable pace. As such, maturation is the ability to meet the demands of one's ever expanding environment. The thinking, priorities and values of an 8 year-old are different from those of a 15 year-old because they are working from very different frames of reference at different times. The demands of family life for a child differ from that of school, the peer group or those of adult institutions. As we grow through each stage these different demands shape us in powerful ways. Whilst we remain entranced by individualism in the West, such personal libertarianism is something of a fantasy. We punish our children for disobedience to the family norms, we exclude pupils for their deviant behaviour, we take disciplinary action against work place radicals and we divorce our hedonistic partners. These social institutions set the perimeters of behaviours as well as the demands of life. We may choose our attachments and commitments within these frameworks, and indeed this expression of personal ethic does individuate us, but we must do so within these institutions of life.

The complexity of these institutions of life increases alongside our capacity to process information at a cognitive level. This does not entail merely knowing more about the world, but demands that we know the world in different ways. At eight we emerge from a sense of self that can be characterised by the concrete and egocentric – 'I am my wants' and move towards the teenage years of the imperial – 'I am my relationships'. By late adolescence we shift again, and begin to define ourselves by our emerging ideological views – 'I am my values'. Just as individual 'wants' become superseded by the group's 'norms', the group mentality becomes usurped by personal 'values'. These 'I am' statements represent the yardsticks by which behaviours, decisions and goals are assessed at each stage. Each stage moves us closer to self-authorship, as we shift away from our families towards our peers, then towards those who share our values and, ultimately, towards our working lives in the institutional world of adults, and the self-defining 'I am what I do'. And for some, they may ultimately live outside adult institutions and have a direct relationship with the world in the final developmental stage of 'I am'.

## Stepping out

These distinct worlds must hold us but also let us go in a timely fashion. Young people find their own place in these worlds through trial and error. They must master the important rehearsals that will prepare them for the next phase of life. Such as a 'best chum' (which teaches about intimate relationships), Saturday jobs (which teach about employment), and holidaying alone or going away to college (which teach about leaving home). Defiance, arguing with parents and kicking against these holding structures are equally important in paving the way for separation. The unsophisticated defiance of the 'terrible two's' marks the first conflict in separating from the mother by saying no. Sibling rivalry separates us from family into peer groups, and the wounding betrayals of the teen years shift us into sub-cultural groups who share and support our values. Well prepared and rehearsed, most young people do not notice their own transformation. These shifting psychological tectonic plates are the growing up in the wonder years. And it is failure to navigate them that is the source of despair. Here conflicts will ensure passage to the next stage of development for the unrehearsed, because it will force separation from the old embeddedness. One needs conflict with one's parents to leave home as much as we might need conflicts in the work place to allow us to separate into new institutional roles. Whilst difficult in the moment, these conflicts when fully realised are creative and liberating forces of development. Hence the value of crises in change.

Adolescents are standing on the cusp of the most profound change they will experience since their birth. Where they move from occupying the cultural institutions that have been provided for them, to having to leave home, school and peer groups and create a world to occupy for themselves. This is in terms of constructing their own family, home, marriage, work and leisure. To do so they must break with the values and aspirations of the family and now project their own ethics onto a possible future which they must establish themselves. This is the greatest developmental shift we make after our birth. The magnitude of such a task is vast. Tellingly, it is during this transition that many young people using drugs fail to transcend, leaving them marooned in the world of drug use and using networks. Certainly, as we get older we become more self-defining and autonomous in our life. But here on the other side of the bridge, young people are anxiously awaiting this shift, which they may or not be fully prepared for. And it is all too easy for adults to forget what life was like back then.

## One for all

For teenagers, the central arena remains their peer groups which come to dominate their lives over the family unit. One has only to recall the obsessions with popularity, rivalries, unrequited crushes and the wounding betrayals of our own teenage years to appreciate how predominant relationships are at this time. Developmental psychologist Judith Harris (1999) has challenged the prevailing wisdom and vicariously supports Kegan's thesis. She suggests that parents are not responsible for the socialisation of children as assumed by psychologist or geneticists. The West is unique in this assumption, but in nearly every culture young people are socialised by their older peers after the age of two. We see this in operation at a neighbourhood level. For example, a migrant family moves to a new country and the parents speak nothing of the adopted tongue. But within six months the children will speak it fluently without formal teaching, due to peer influence. Likewise, when it comes to behaviours, cultural theorist Malcom Gladwell (2000) has concluded, from the results of antisocial behaviour studies, 'a child is better off in a good neighbourhood and a troubled family than he or she is in a troubled neighbourhood with a good family'.

Children soon learn that what they can do in the home and in the playground is very different. They also police a strict boundary between the two. The world may filter into the home, but home life will not percolate into the peer group.

As every schoolteacher knows, young people break off into smaller peer groups by the age of 12 and start forging bonds with individuals similar to them. So the 'brains', the 'sportos', the 'fashion victims' and the 'wasters' soon cluster together. If parents wish to control their children at this stage of development, they must exert sanctions on who they are hanging out with. Within these units, peer pressure is not a malign force towards mischief but a drive to participate in these all important sub-units. And, just as peer pressure endorses certain risk taking behaviour, so it also legislates against others. For example, it is commonly the case that smoking cannabis is viewed as fine but using heroin is ruled out entirely. Yet, as two researchers who studied adolescent drug users have noted, 'The fact that peer pressure can aid adolescents in *controlling* and *abandoning* deviant activities and in the maturation process is ignored in popular thinking about peer pressure and . . . in most research literature' (Glassner and Loughlin, 1990):

## Different, like everyone else

We cannot divorce behaviours from the context of the groups in which they are enacted because the peer group is the source of identity at this stage. Studies have repeatedly highlighted that the pattern of close peers' drug use has more impact on young people's consumption than ethnicity, parental consumption, religious back-ground, personality, environment or gender (see Gonzalez, 1989; Jessor and Jessor, 1977; Kandal, 1980; Oetting and Beauvais, 1986). Furthermore, the behaviours of these groups become increasingly exaggerated when contact is made with other groups, even if they are demographically identical, to preserve identity (Harris, 1999). Thus girls act more feminine in the company of male groups, and males act more macho. This also means, within our clusters, the nerds get nerdier, the brains get brainer and the wasters get excluded.

As young people's goals differ radically from those of adults, the biggest mistake is to impose adult values on them at this stage. Young people's world view is dominated by the importance of relationships, whereas, for adults, it is social institutions. Young people identify themselves as different by being in conflict with the adult world view. This is part of their growth process of separation from imposed values to the accession of their own. Besides, young people are punished precisely for acting like adults, an irony not lost on them.

Young people do not want to be adults. They want to be like their older peers within their sub-faction – the ones who, in Kegan's terms, have shifted into the next world view and enjoy the privileges and personal freedoms that it brings. Most drug treatment programmes forget this and are too mature in their design, well ahead of adolescents' natural development. Young people can never be 'instant' adults but must work their way through each vital stage towards adulthood. And the cultivation of values within a sub-faction is an important phase.

## Back to basics

When we overlay these principle ideas of developmental psychology on the pattern of youth drug use, critical issues for both prevention and treatment are raised, which are lost in the moral stampede. We have to accept that drug use has a functional role in young people's lives. The fact that the majority of people take drugs because they are fun, help them bond through shared experience and provide social ceremonies is a stark reality which is wholly lost in drug prevention messages and betrays the moralistic bias of adults. The latter instigates immediate rejection by young people and imbues drug use with the mystique of defiance.

Homing in on how the tobacco and alcohol industries persuade young people to use their drugs has generated a greater reaction in terms of drug prevention – for instance asking young people what message they think cigarette advertising is trying to get across (McMurran, 1997). Self-generated answers such as 'They are trying to make us think we'll look cool if we smoke', are more effective in leading young people to question the validity of such an assumption or defy it. I would suggest that getting groups of young people to compare themselves to imagined groups of heroin using peers would also be effective, creating a clear separation between themselves and the heroin using groups, and strengthening their own group norms.

Drug use is not simply a matter of individual choice but is made meaningful within the group and social context. A degree of intoxication is a state of mind most young people must learn to manage as a key facet of social interaction, regardless of whether this is by culturally sanctioned drugs like alcohol or illicit ones which will remain widely available. Family upbringing does have a role in this. As we have seen, moderate using parents raise moderately using children. Beyond the reach of supervised parental control though, intoxication is learned by trial and error. Young people approach substances with sets of expectations of what the substance will do for them. They experience an intoxication event and then make sense of this, according to their expectations. That which does not fit is excluded. It is only with the experience of negative social realities, that cannot be discounted, that mediate the exceptions (Goldman et al., 1993). However, within the peer group, use may create normative fallacies. If everyone within the group is acting out, it normalises shameful or deviant behaviour. Focusing on ways in which heavy intoxication can negatively impact upon prized relationships, such as dating, would also be likely to moderate usage more than strict edicts to abstain. However, if peer education programmes are to work, they must draw upon young people from a broad section of social clusters, and their target audience should be younger siblings rather than peers, who will already be looking up to those who have shifted into the next world view.

However, even when there is forethought in drug management, it can still be overruled by the peer group. Drug education programmes which actually recognise the positive value of intoxicants and their function as social lubricants, expose the realities behind overtly positive expectations of drugs as mood control and which build skills in managing these states of mind, have higher impact than the hope of immunising young people against a social reality. Indeed, it was positive outcomes from this approach that inspired the most successful drug prevention programme, Life Skills Training (Botvin et al., 1992).

## Job seekers' allowance

Life Skills Training, developed by psychologist Professor Gilbert Botvin, challenges the 'normative fallacy' that all young people are taking drugs, and take them to excess, by helping young people understand why it is that some people take drugs. His programme does not focus on drugs themselves but teaches a wide range of general life skills, such as managing relationships, personal development, goal setting, etc. Issues such as low self-esteem, and lack of refusal skills and self-confidence are addressed not as an end in themselves but as obstacles to the successful deployment of these life skills. Evaluation research found that nine per cent of Botvin's group smoked, compared with 12 per cent of a control group, and a three per cent cannabis prevalence compared with six per cent in the control group (Stothard and Ashton, 2000). Bigger differences, in favour of the programme, were found in polydrug use, though alcohol consumption was unaffected. These gains seem modest but are significant in light of other drug prevention programmes' failure to produce any positive results at all.

Botvin's programmes were also significant in that they recognised that, within age bands, different peer groups existed. When they tailored the programme to the higher risk groups, modest gains were made across a number of areas, including drinking, despite making no references to intoxicants at all. With the higher risk groups, there was, however, no effect on cannabis use. I would suggest this might be because cannabis use is a cultural norm among the ethnic groups which made up the higher risk groups. (Similarly, across the mixed groups, where drinking is a cultural norm, alcohol consumption did not fall.) Perhaps this is why Botvin's life skill programmes are the most successful drug education programmes available. His programmes do not discuss drugs other than to challenge the thinly veiled adult concerns embedded in so many other programmes. Instead, they teach young people the life skills to move into the adult world, enabling them to make the transition and construct their own institutional life.

It appears far more apposite to teach young people about the nature of growing up than the nature of illicit pharmacology. What Botvin did recognise was that, in the high risk groups, the disadvantages of poverty was a serious obstacle to classroom based prevention. This raises the same concerns about young people at highest risk of developing problematic use and their treatment being too narrow to be effective.

## Them and us

Reviewing the demographic spread of drug using patterns, it is difficult to ignore the fact that most people age out of this behaviour. As we have seen, research with 'aged out' populations makes it clear that drug use becomes crowded out by more meaningful activities. Interviewees report that jobs, relationships and children become more central in their lives (Erickson and Hadaway, 1989). This occurs across the twenties, the point Kegan describes as a shift from the idealistic self to an institutional self, where one joins the labour market and engages with other social constructs such as marriage, mortgages and the creation of a family unit. Within this shift of context, drugs become less meaningful.

However, for the shift to occur, people must have left their idealistic phase, have appropriate opportunities to both separate and re-embed themselves into the next cultural structure as they develop, and have viable preparedness and the self-belief to operate in this new world. Life Skills Training can give young people the tools to assist in this but does not address the 'social-economic bridges' people also need. When we look at young people who experience drug problems, those with mental ill health are 13 times more likely to have drug and alcohol problems (Rorstad et al., 1996), whilst 63 per cent of socially excluded young people will have tried cannabis compared to 25 per cent of those in school. A further 29 per cent will have used class A drugs and 61 per cent will have used class B, compared to five per cent and 15 per cent of school attendees respectively (Evans, 2002). Emotional disadvantage and poverty are major factors. Social exclusion removes the preparations for life.

In short, these individuals do not have the viable skills or self-belief to operate in a more adult world and as a result have no means to separate from the contexts of family or peer relationships. They are caught between an old world that can no longer satisfy and a new world they cannot attain. The function of drug using shifts from pleasure seeking and shared group experience to becoming the only purposeful activity in these people's lives. It gives them a reason to get up, something to do (raise money, score drugs), others to associate with in a shared pursuit and the reward of a chemically induced mood state which is expected to mimic a sense of satisfaction. Addiction is the sanctuary for cultural orphans.

*Drug Induced*

Traditionally our approach has been to exclude these people from mainstream education and clump them with peers from the same sub-faction, thus enlarging the very group dynamic we hoped to abate, deepening exclusion and cementing people into problematic lifestyles. Or these young people are retained even more tightly by the concerns of the parent, who try to rescue them from their crises. This only serves to keep the young person from having to take control for themselves. In other words we trap them in the old world. The greater this holding back, the greater the conflict needed for the young person to break out of this old way of being, thus amplifying problematic behaviours until the crisis point is reached. And as we have seen the crisis is the engine for change.

## Brave young world

These were the critical issues I felt needed to be addressed when asked to design a national pilot relapse prevention programme for young people. Firstly it was important to recognise that not all young people with problem drug use are ready for the deep change we explored in Chapter 6. Change occurs in key stages which we will explore in Chapter 8 (see also Connors et al., 2001). By advertising and networking, we ended up with 11 people aged between 18 and 25 who felt they had an issue with substance abuse and agreed to join our pilot programme. Some came from a probation hostel and had been convicted many times for 'acquisitive' crimes. Others had severe mental health problems and had been hospitalised on one or more occasions. To assess their readiness for the programme, colleagues and I used the Inventory of Drug-Taking Situations developed by the Addiction Research Foundation based in Toronto (Annis et al., 1996). This questionnaire enables assessment of both client readiness for change and specific individual relapse triggers.

What was significant in the assessment of our young people is that they did not score highly on negative mood states that would indicate pathology, but did score highly on positive mood states and social pressure, highlighting the role of peer group and expectancy in use. Furthermore, their life stories had much in common. Many of these young people couldn't cope with leaving home, whether to go to college or elsewhere. When their old world of peers disappeared, and the new one of entering into groups which cohere around values did not take. Problems appeared twofold. Firstly, many had been unsuccessful in managing previous adjustments as a result of trauma, abuse or deprivation. Whilst others had a skills deficit which prevented them from meeting the demands of nascent adult life due to social exclusion. These young people had fallen down the gap between worlds, where the drift into drugs had become their only focus.

## Cultural therapy

The treatment element of the pilot programme attempts to address these deficits in several ways. In the first phase of treatment, we offer a short cognitive behaviour programme for managing drug use, cravings and lapse experiences. The second phase addresses broader life skills such as relationships, goal setting, identity and emotional management. We supported each young person to re-engage with their families after years of estrangement. The tacit aim within these groups is to foster the individual's 'idealistic' self, to cultivate personal values which are greater than their peer group's norms. We implemented a buddy system of mutual support to foster intimate relationships beyond the peer group, equivalent to a 'best friend' in the natural course of development. The group itself needed to cohere around a shared norm and then police each other in remaining within this norm, which was the commitment to change. For this reason, it was emphasised that all attendees would be expected to return and assist in future programmes. The project was to be as much theirs as ours, and we considered they had an obligation towards those that followed them to preserve these values.

It was equally important that we got past the 'autistic' vision of so much psychotherapy and psychology that suggests that people are independent minds, divorced from the social world they occupy. We tried to recreate the 'cultural therapy' that was missing in these young people's lives. So we put in place basic skills training, work placements and individual and team building tasks to replicate preparations that so many had missed, to assist them into the next phase of their development.

Inevitably, we had to expect conflicts during this process. In traditional approaches, conflict is seen as negative and becomes the excuse to kick people out of treatment. But these young people need a framework to kick against as much as they need it to hold them. Dealing with conflict directly, by helping individuals to look at what purpose their aggression, deviance or defiance was really serving and how to manage their needs more constructively has been an integral part of the programme. As such, it is a treatment strategy to engage and support the person that each of them is becoming.

The early outcomes were extremely positive. Our drop out rate was low and our first round of evaluations demonstrated improvements in all key areas of functioning. Our community based pilot did not impose total abstinence, which has a negative impact on outcomes of young people (Annis et al., 1996). And young people are not removed for lapsing, providing they do not use whilst attending the programme. Instead we expect them to disclose and use these experiences as an opportunity for them to learn. Residential treatment programmes achieve better immediate outcomes, but these decay once people leave and face real temptations, which they have been protected from (Marlatt and Gordon, 1985). Conversely, addressing these issues in the community develops increasing self-confidence in managing risk situations which means outcomes snowball upward over two years (Marlatt, 1996). Lapse frequency has significantly decreased across the course of the pilot, urine analysis, which is routinely carried out in probation hostels, showed that even the hostel residents were drug free on completion. Our biggest concern, however, was always one of housing which was tremendously difficult to sustain for young people, often they were discharged into the community with nowhere to live, thus significantly increasing their risk of reverting to living in squalid housing with other users.

The programme was designed as a community response to these young people's drug problems. As such, we relied heavily on the community to work with us in re-integrating these young people back in to a full life. Without these broader supports such as housing, training, education, health and employment, these young people will remain vulnerable to relapse. Indeed, in a conference organised for professionals by this group, they themselves identified these critical barriers to their development. However, in accordance with Marlatt's predication, two years after the end of the pilot, these young people have continued to make great strides in their own development. Despite a return to use at the end of the structured programme, they have returned to engage in treatment, with the majority now clean in the community and the remainder making good progress in supported arenas.

Research clearly indicates that employment is the most important force in creating sustainable outcomes for young people (Lipsey, 1999). The shift to employment breaks the monopoly of the peer group and provides a means to finance alternative sources of satisfaction. Drug use remains a high impact, low skill pursuit against a backdrop of high skill, low impact rewards of the modern day market place. The preparations of apprenticeships for trade have been replaced by the higher demands for qualifications which outpace the expectations of many young people. Manual and semi-skilled labour markets have evaporated, taking traditional social and gender roles with them. The anticipated life route for many of these young people no longer exists. It is little wonder that problematic drug use correlates with unemployment, poverty, dysfunctional families and prison incarceration (Bickel and DeGrandpre, 1995). Scaling the maturation ladder in a society in economic flux is difficult enough, but many young people simply do not even have a ladder.

## Conclusion

Adult approaches to youth drugs' issues share one central problem. They remain adult. If we wish to make a sincere attempt to insulate young people from the real dangers that drugs can cause, we must do so from within their world view, not ours. Drugs prevention should not be a vehicle to satisfy our agendas but must be directly relevant to young people's own concerns. Without relevancy to their world, our efforts will remain meaningless. Ultimately outcomes for young people's treatment programmes will be determined by the tension between the efficacy of the programme in providing them with the lost rehearsals for life, against the overwhelming feelings of excluded young people when returning to mainstream cultural institutions after many years of absence. As such, so many of the problems they face are the result of social exclusion not drug use in itself. Yet drugs have remained a scapegoat for social ills which arise from social reform's inability to address broader concerns such as emotional and social deprivation. Treatment must address the full expanse of the human experience and help restore the life course that has been diverted by these forces. Only then can young people hope to manifest their potential, whether through the maturational process or by a decisive act of will.

Adapted from 'Young, Gifted and Blocked', *Human Givens: Radical Psychology Today*. Summer 2000

# Chapter 8

# Well Intentioned Change

*I'm cleaning up and I'm moving on, going straight and choosing life. I am looking forward to it already. I am going to be just like you: the job, the family, the fucking big television, the washing machine, the car, the compact disc and electrical tin opener, good heath, low cholesterol, dental insurance, mortgage, starter home, leisure wear, luggage, three piece suite, DIY, game shows, junk food, children, walks in the park, nine to five, good at golf, washing the car, choice of sweaters, family Christmas, indexed pension, tax exemption, clearing the gutters, getting by, looking ahead, to the day that you die.*

Irvine Welsh

Change is at the heart of every treatment enterprise, and particularly so in treatment for addiction. But very few approaches attempt to understand the process or consider the ramifications. As a result, treatment can become a hit and miss affair, where clients happen, or not, to come across the right therapist at the right point in their change process. It is vital that understanding of the nature of change and its impact on interventions is pulled into the therapeutic arena, for the benefit of clients and counsellors alike. As we have seen, individuals may mature, evolve or leap out of addictive lifestyles via a deep personal revelation of a spiritual nature.

All of these processes do inform treatment to varying degrees. Many users cease use because they simply evolved into other activities. Others feel they are becoming increasingly adrift from their life journey which prompts a deep re-evaluation. Whilst for some, the inexplicable spiritual reawakening, which defies our current understanding of human change, spirits them to higher concerns. This may explain why non-treatment groups consistently do better than treatment groups. It is only when clients are stuck in the process of change that they seek out professional help or are coerced into treatment. This leaves them only one option, and that is to take it upon themselves to transform their lives by stint of their own personal efforts. Difficulty in managing intentional change is therefore a crucial issue for all treatment modalities and one which demands deeper attention.

## Intentional change

Empirical findings about the nature of intentional change have been available since the mid-1980s, and have been widely adopted in the addiction field. However, this has tended towards assisting the client to recognise where they are in their own process in the hope that this is illuminating for them in itself. Alas, however, the significance for practitioners – as a framework within which to integrate relevant therapeutic responses – has hardly been appreciated at all.

The two psychologists who carried out the groundbreaking work were Prochaska and DiClemente (1984). They were increasingly dissatisfied with dogmatism within psychotherapy which propounded individual mechanisms of change but failed to explore the experience of change itself. Whilst counselling has fragmented into over 400 different schools, Prochaska's review of 24 leading psychotherapies identified that there were only actually nine change mechanisms which could be drawn upon (see Table 1).

## Transcending theory

Prochaska and DiClemente took their exploration further by studying individuals engaging in intentional change and charting what happened. They based this study on a group of smokers and found that intentional change was not sudden but moved through clear, sequential stages of self-awareness, which they called the 'cycle of change'. Each stage of the model describes a very different emotional mindset, level of awareness and goal orientation. Initially people have no awareness of the implications of their behaviour. In pre-contemplation, it is important to deploy approaches which build relationships and raise people's consciousness of the problems. Accepting drug use as a choice and finding opportunities to discuss harm reduction often raises individuals' concerns about behaviour. After all, there is only so much that can be reduced. It may also provide an opportunity to reality check the expectations of the user with the actuality of their use. All too frequently a user's expectations of consumption rarely figure in the descriptions of using experiences and this creates scope to develop this discrepancy and challenge positive expectancies which can drive use. A positive alliance allows these messages to be delivered without the person feeling judged and rejected out of hand. This will often prompt contemplation of current behaviour.

Contemplative clients are considering change. This can be cultivated through greater awareness of problems connected with their use, as well as the increasing external pressures caused by their use and/or exclusion. As a result they may be close, or nearing, the crisis moment when the pressure of continued use become untenable in light of mounting pressures on health, family, relationships, sense of isolation and life course disparity. But, as the problematic behaviours have performed some function in their lives, they will have ambivalent feelings about abandoning them. To attempt a global revision of lifestyle, and abandon all that is known and familiar for an uncertain reward is not an easy decision. So, although drug users experience increasing anxiety about their lifestyle and want to change, ambivalence paralyses this process. Their underlying anxiety needs to be enhanced and their ambivalent feelings resolved.

Considering the ideas from maturational development we looked at in the last chapter, we may also see contemplation from a richer perspective. Typically, it is seen as a cognitive behavioural model. But research among natural drug remitters highlights a deeper existential process. Ambivalence is a defining feature of contemplation that both initiates consideration of change and paralyses this process. And as Miller and Rollnick (1991) observe 'In many cases, *working with the ambivalence is working with the heart of the problem.*' Yet we never ask, where does this internal voice that questions the current lifestyle and ethics emerge? I would suggest that the experience of ambivalence towards use that initiates the process of change represents an internal dialogue between the established self and an emergent 'maturational' one, one that gains a bird's eye view of the problems that drugs are generating in the individual's life. This emergent view is the more mature self, with a different meaning and valuing system, casting doubt upon current behaviour that no longer satisfies. And we are unable to take a bird's eye view of our behaviour without becoming that bird's eye view: because we cannot enter into old, once unquestioned, behaviours without questioning them. Hence intentional change and maturational change may intersect.

Through resolving the intrapersonal conflicts, people can enter *preparation* for change. Preparation is a problematic stage. Originally absent in the first Cycle of Change models, it became known as 'determination' and was later dubbed 'preparation'. The standard definition is that the client will change within 30 days. This appears to be a prophecy rather than an intentional state of mind as described in the other stages. This lack of definition may arise from Prochaska and DiClemente's subjects who are smokers, and smokers are not exiled from their lives as drug users are. Klingemann's (1991) research into the natural remission of problematic drug users demonstrates two powerful changes do occur here which redefine our current understanding. The first is that the *external* pressures on contemplators to change are *internalised* once the decision to change is made. The individual must now confront the personal struggle to defeat oneself and the ingrained behaviours. The well rehearsed strategies to manage external pressures are of no use when confronting oneself. And secondly, those in 'preparation' isolate themselves from their peer groups. Separation from this culture of identity is essential if a new identity is to develop and find expression in more fulfilling networks of relationships. Those who do not separate have a very poor prognosis whilst these attachments remain equal, if not more important, than the unknown rewards of change. And nobody will put a significant effort into change to be worse off than they are. This demands more than planning strategies such as exploring appropriate detoxification options and post-detox treatment plans. It demands the cultivating of a future sense of who they will become instead.

Once this future orientation is established in the client's perception of themselves, they must turn these intentions into *action* and implement the changes. Treatment only works well when the client feels that the journey towards achieving personal

**Table 1  Comparison of mechanism of change**

| Process | Goals | Services |
|---|---|---|
| | **Pre-contemplation-contemplation** | |
| Consciousness raising | Increasing information about the behaviour through observation, interpretations, reading, as well as the nature of problems as well as how you can avoid pitfalls in changing them. | Needle exchange schemes<br>Drop-in<br>Detached work<br>Advice and information |
| Social liberation | Avoiding or controlling external factors that are not conducive to the old behaviour, such as non-smoking areas. Campaigning for rights as individuals which demand change in the social environment. | Non-specialist services that may encounter problematic use such as probation services, social services, health services |
| | **Contemplation-preparation** | |
| Self-revaluation | Assessing feelings and thoughts about self with respect to the problem and the kind of life you want for yourself. What are the emotional or rational losses and gains in change or staying the same? | Semi-structured, rapid access services<br>Drop-in<br>Needle exchange<br>Outreach<br>Assessments |
| Emotional arousal | Powerful and deep emotional experiences which raise an emotional awareness and catharsis regarding the problem. Often induced by crises or tragedies. | One-to-one sessions<br>Low intensity group work for those considering change<br>Community prescribing services |

## Preparation-action

| | | |
|---|---|---|
| Commitment | Once you have chosen to change, one's preparedness to make the private and then the public commitment to act. Increases pressure on oneself to succeed and achieve one's goals. | Assessment for aftercare Referral for intensive treatment interventions Aftercare planning |

## Action-maintenance

| | | |
|---|---|---|
| Reward | Rewarding self or being rewarded by others for making change. This can include self-praise, gifts, access to alternative enrichment or other positive experiences. Punishments do not work well as an alternative. | Community detoxification Symptom management detoxification In-patient detoxification Residential treatment Structured day care |
| Environmental control | Deliberately avoiding triggers that elicit problem behaviours or removing the means to access them such as getting rid of drug paraphernalia, alcohol or avoiding other users. | Housing Rebuilding social support Family |
| Helping relationships | Enlisting the help of people that care for you. This may demand letting people know what we need from them. This may be from professionals but not necessarily. | Self-help groups Skills training Employment |
| Countering | Substitute alternative behaviours for problem behaviours. When faced with cravings the user may use exercise as a means of detracting from them, smokers may chew gum instead or people with weight problems might eat fruit. | Specialist no-drug specific services (forensic psychiatry, Hep C, HIV, liver specialists) |

goals is relevant to their needs and sense of themselves. Therefore they need to be offered a pro-active role in formulating the treatment plans. Action demands contingency management and the bolstering of self-belief the most important predictor of outcome. Self-belief not only includes people's anticipation of their own performance but their persistence in overcoming obstacles and setbacks. Even if we take the worse case scenario that withdrawal from a drug like heroin is only as bad as a dose of the flu, it is not the desperately unmanageability of symptoms that is undermining the process. After all, flu is not the end of the world. It is the erosion of self-belief to persist, rather than the symptoms, that becomes the critical issue in undermining this stage of change. We do know that withdrawal symptoms are actually very elastic. Alleviating negative expectations can do much to lighten this process. One woman who was withdrawing from heroin rang me to complain of stomach cramps and pleaded for methadone. I asked her what else was going on at the time and found that she had just had a row with her boyfriend, who had never been a user and whose attitude was not helping. I asked her, 'What would he need to know to be able to help you?' After we had discussed how they might manage this jointly, I enquired, 'By the way, how are the stomach cramps?' To her surprise, they had disappeared.

During maintenance of the new behaviour, stimulus control, social liberation and a helping relationship are required. Using stress inoculation techniques such as teaching clients to anticipate risks, learn coping skills in advance and rehearse them first (Marlatt and Gordon, 1985), help them to manage the early risk of relapse (see Chapter 12). Again, people's confidence is low at this stage. Abandoning drug use will create a void in their life as both the purposeful activity and prior 'active' relationships are shorn away by quitting use. For many, learning the skills to meet the demands of the everyday become an important priority in order to lessen the overwhelming feeling of the new and complex demands that they will now be subjected to.

Again, in drug using populations we see a bigger shift in self-identity occur than in our dependant smokers. Klingemann (1992) identified in detail what many natural remission studies also highlight. We see in the maintenance phases an emergence of a new perspective on life, often expressed as a new set of values. They re-embed in new groups of identity, with new totems and new pro-social values. To manage this successfully is one of the biggest predictors of treatment outcome (see Chapter 13). Furthermore, many treated and untreated users either become workers in the field or post-materialists in some kind of fringe mystical or religious beliefs. They never subscribe to the orthodoxy of mainstream culture but find a sub-strata of identity within it. In other words they subscribe to new cultures of identity where their past experience becomes the totem of identity rather than active drug use. The past purpose of drug use, now becomes the means to support a new present purpose of change. Our choices are limited within this, to joining cultures of identity that express an ethic that we can subscribe too. In drug users what we see is that change involves the creation of a new identity, a more mature self which re-embeds itself in pro-social groups. Interestingly alcohol users who face these dilemmas later in life do not overhaul their personality in such a dramatic fashion. They experience two disadvantages. The later onset of use means that they experience greater difficultly in changing personality, which is harder to do post age thirty (Sugarman, 2000). And additionally, it is easier to escape the extra-cultural shadow society of drug use in a way it is not possible to escape the inter-cultural use of alcohol.

Whilst maintenance needs to focus on sustaining the change in behaviour, this may mean choosing to enter residential treatment, community programmes or take up other options that they feel meets their needs more fully. However, it is important to recognise, and normalise, that many treatment and non-treatment seekers relapse into former coping strategies and drug use. Prochaska and DiClemente's initial group of smokers relapsed six or seven times before they were able to stay stopped. A relapse was therefore an unpleasant but essential part of the process for them. At a statistical level it has proved difficult to understand which mechanisms might be most useful to the client – and the initial research on change only made sense once they were removed as a sub-group (Prochaska et al., 1994). If lapse occurs, causing feelings of failure and an inability to change, relapse may follow. And when all the means for success have been put at your disposal and you still fail, this may even deepen the despair felt, encouraging more use to sedate these negative feelings.

A handwritten letter to invite back someone who has lapsed back into services or support can be a powerful hook to reconnect with the individual that feels they have let you down somehow. With one heroin using client who also experienced depression and agoraphobia, I would write and enclose a sae, paper and pen. She would always write back, welcomed it as an opportunity to stay in touch, and knew that I was not rejecting her because of a lapse. Those who have relapsed need help to re-evaluate their decision to change and become aware of the specific skills deficits which undermined the process. What might have been viewed as a process of failure can then be re-framed as a failure to process learning. Unless we can represent lapse as a change episode; a partial success that can be built upon, clients' disappointment may drive them into black and white thinking, interpreting the lapse as complete failure and spiralling back into uncontrollable drug use.

## Working with what works

As Prochaska and DiClemente pointed out, no single 'leading' therapy approach encompasses the full spectrum of mechanisms of change, most drawing upon two or three at best. It is essential that therapy is as cognitively complex as the clients it professes to help.

Unsurprisingly, then, treatments that focus on specific areas appear to be more effective than generalised approaches and, in developing counselling and treatment programmes, it is important to draw upon behaviour specific interventions (McGuire, 1995). Once we gain insight into the process of change, it becomes clear that it is not possible to work with a client in a manner which does not meet their current needs, levels of awareness or readiness to change. All too often, treatment providers and therapists opt for a 'one size fits all' approach, generating high rates of drop out, which occurs mostly in the first two weeks of treatment. It appears that clients pick up on the discrepancy between treatment and need far more quickly than counsellors do, and respond in the most emphatic way. As a result we must match the intervention to where the individual is in the cycle of change in order to address concerns, needs and goals that are relevant to them. When I hear individuals complain of bad treatment episodes, invariably the counsellor is not doing anything wrong as such. They are just not doing it in the right place. Talking to a contemplative user about how to manage change will alienate them very quickly.

If we look at the mechanisms of change identified by Prochaska and DiClemente, we can see that the pre-contemplation stage is the time to try consciousness raising. For this I would use Rogerian listening skills and harm reduction strategies. At the contemplation stage, the emphasis needs to be on re-evaluation of existing goals and beliefs. Motivational interviewing techniques are effective in initiating powerful change in alcoholics as well as increasing treatment compliance in drug users (Miller and Rollnick, 2002). During the preparation stage, people need help to rid themselves of negative self-definitions, for which I use solution focused therapy techniques. For maintaining treatment gains, stress inoculation has been found by the Addiction Research Foundation in Toronto to be 30 per cent more effective than traditional counselling styles (Annis et al., 1991). The cycle of change is therefore transtheoretical. It provides a framework whereby different treatment approaches can be seen to be appropriate during different stages of change. Other interventions could be deployed here, provided they contain the correct mechanisms for the stage.

## Case Study: Robert and the cycle of change

Robert became increasing depressed after his marriage broke up, and his use of alcohol and amphetamine began to spiral out of control. Soon he switched to injecting the drug and signed up for the needle exchange at the local drug agency, so that he could swap dirty needles for clean ones. In these first visits I managed to build up an alliance with Robert. He disclosed some of his history in these brief meetings and began to ask about safer drug use. The rapport we had built up and the harm reduction advice I gave him raised his awareness of the risks of his drug use in a non-judgemental way. Soon he asked for an appointment to discuss change.

In this first session Robert recognised the need for change but felt that he could just quit and did not need support. We agreed a plan and a means of staying in contact if it should not succeed. He made an attempt to stop and sustained it for two weeks before lapsing and returning to the drug project. He was more depressed and his drug use now felt uncontrollable. Using motivational interviewing I amplified his concerns about using drugs by asking him what he feared would happen if he did not change. We also explored his ambivalence: the drug was helping him manage feelings about his marriage break up but was also self-destructive. As a result of weighing this up, he made a stronger commitment to change. Using the solution focused therapy techniques, I helped Robert construct a vision of the life he wanted for himself. Together we planned how to achieve this.

Robert decided that a traditional residential treatment programme would be his best option. He first enrolled on our community treatment programme, however, which focuses on preparation for change. To assist with the detoxification process, we also explored his expectations of withdrawal symptoms, and whether these were caused by the drug, low self-belief or anxiety. He then went to the rehabilitation centre of his choice but two months later was back at the project, using again. His counsellor at the rehabilitation centre had discharged him for not making adequate progress on resolving issues regarding his divorce.

Robert felt very depressed and defeated. The counsellor had given him the message that not even a rehabilitation centre could help him because he was so damaged by his relationship break up. He was a 'hopeless case'. We reappraised his reasons for deciding to quit using drugs and his hopes for the future, and started to rebuild his shattered self-belief. This inspired a new resolve. Robert decided to enter our community based counselling programme. Here we identified a hierarchy of risk situations and his current range of coping strategies. We set tasks for him to confront the least risky situation first and began to build his confidence in managing more difficult ones. There were lapses but these were seen as part of the learning process. We also explored how he could enrich his life in new ways. He began playing his guitar again and volunteered for work with an animal sanctuary. A year later, Robert was still clean, has expanded his work in animal welfare and now plays guitar for a band.

## The problem with common factors

There is a general trend in counselling towards *common factors approaches*, in which the similarities shared by different counselling orientations (e.g. quality of the relationship, frequency and length of sessions) are seen as the significant elements in prompting change. Sol Garfield (1992), professor emeritus of psychology at Washington University, pioneered this idea of distilling what works across all modalities. Yet he also said, 'I prefer patients who have "reasonably" clear problems, are not psychotically impaired, exhibit some degree of anxiety or depression, appear to want to work on their problems, and show no serious occupational or social disorganisation' – an observation which makes it clear that he is most comfortable working with people in the preparation stage of the cycle of change and are not residing in the shadow society of social exclusion.

In brief solution focused therapy, the rise to prominence of which owes much to Garfield's (1992) work amongst others, clients stand on the threshold of having to turn the intentions which emerge and are resolved in contemplation, and thought through in preparation into action. And measuring a shift in behaviour is much easier than measuring a shift in intentional states of mind. Solution focused approaches work well with clients in preparation, who are likely to implement change within the next 30 days, but do not, it seems to me, seem able to address the needs of those who have not yet reached this stage of readiness.

The transtheoretical approach places a much greater onus on counsellors to develop a wider skills base and diverse treatment strategies. At the very least, it requires them to recognise the stages of change at which they are, and aren't, proficient at working with clients. For example, a counsellor who is oriented towards action will find pre-contemplative clients frustrating. Some drug worker posts only enable people to work with clients in a specific stage of change. A relapse avoidance worker, for instance, only supports those in maintenance, whilst GP liaison workers are concerned with those in contemplation. These workers need to be expert in specific areas of change. Whereas other workers, on prison wings, working with young people or in generic services, need to be proficient at working with any stage of the cycle.

## The effect on compliance

Transtheoretical counselling challenges key assumptions about addiction that traditional approaches have created. Firstly the model demands we make a key shift in thinking. We will never work with the client's problems, whether they be addiction or otherwise. We will only ever work with their attitudes to their problems which remain somewhat invariant. Secondly, the cycle of change describes dependency not as an entrenched biological disorder but a process of adaptation. The role of the therapist is not to cure the client but to accelerate the pace and efficiency with which they pass through each stage. Traditionally it was believed that clients had to reach rock bottom before they would initiate change. However, research indicates that not all users need to, and that these 'high bottom users' can be helped to turn their lives around before real crises overwhelm them. As such it becomes a whole populations approach, not just for those who have decided to change.

Within traditional frameworks of treatment, a client's inability to comply with treatment was seen as a denial of their state of dependency, rather than their being in a lower order of readiness. This resulted in confrontative approaches which generated high drop-out rates from treatment (Miller, 1998). The cycle of change shifts the non-compliance balance towards the service provider. Non-compliance is not a symptom of a mythical illness but of an inappropriate treatment regime. Rigid treatment models which do not meet the client's changing needs are simply attempting to hammer increasingly round pegs into square holes. One of the tests conducted to establish the validity of the cycle of change model was used to predict drop-out in programmes which did not compensate for the fluid nature of change.

It did so with 93 per cent accuracy. The practitioner thus becomes a consultant in the process, 'a midwife at the birth of change' (Miller and Rollnick, 1991). We must focus on providing an appropriate, quality intervention, in a collaborative and supportive environment. What clients may choose to do within this framework remains their individual responsibility.

## Paradoxical reactions to change

The transtheoretical approach has been applied with a high degree of success to a wide variety of fields of human behaviour, including health, mental health, weight control, offending and exercise amongst others (Prochaska and DiClemente, 1992). However, the approach has not been without its detractors and these analyses are insightful. An attempt to quantify the statistical validity of the model highlighted a continuum towards change, rather than discrete hops from one stage to another.

The process did not appear to be purely sequential (Budd and Rollnick, 1996; see also Sutton, 1996).

Contemplative clients often revert back to pre-contemplation. Why this regression should occur raises interesting questions for drug treatment services. One possibility is a paradoxical reaction to change: when clients seek treatment, their drug use escalates. We have already identified ambivalence as a powerful roadblock to change. Ambivalence may generate a deep anxiety, amplified by whether individuals believe that they have the potential to manage change effectively. Those with high self-belief tend towards anxiety reducing strategies and amend problematic behaviours. Those with low self-belief chose fear reducing strategies, using more drugs to smother the fear that change is not manageable.

Ambivalence may also be situational. As we have seen in the work of Falk (1981) this occurs when individuals want to escape their situation but have limited access to anything better, so vacillate in a displacement activity whilst waiting for the balance to tip one way or the other. An impoverished drug using lifestyle versus the offer of hope at the end of long waiting lists may create such vacillation, inducing compulsive usage in the interim. Certainly, individuals placed on waiting lists do just that, they wait and make no change. Situational ambivalence can be dealt with by abating the negative forces or increasing the positive ones. Flexible services, where quick appointments can be made to look at ambivalence and goal setting, can help initiate the process of change and begin to tip the balance. This can be furthered by improving the quality of individuals' lives in general, introducing a wider source of positive reinforcement.

## Conclusion

Prochaska once asserted that psychotherapy is probably 10 to 20 years away from its heyday. It is a sad irony that psychotherapy seems so resistant to development.

In a recent discussion about accreditation with a national counselling accreditation body, I was informed I would not be eligible as the treatment approaches I employed were not counselling. On further investigation, it turned out simply that they had never heard of them. All too often, research findings are ignored or perceived as personal criticism rather than an opportunity to enrich the practice of therapists. Psychosocial treatments remain in their infancy. So much potential will remain untapped, and so many needs will remain unmet, if therapists are determined to keep them there. Whilst robust and emergent findings from research are not percolating in to the field of practice. Bringing these two aspects together is not easy but can be done in the revision of the cultures of counselling practice within an organisation. And exploring how these can and have converged is what we shall explore next.

Based on 'Addiction: Treatment and Change', *Human Givens: Journal of Radical Psychology.* October 2001

# Chapter 9

# Counselling, Outcomes and Other Sacred Cows

*I'm close to giving up on my therapy. I'll give it another fifteen years and if that doesn't do it, I'm quitting!*

Woody Allen

The talking cure faces its greatest challenge yet – to prove its own worth. Academics, purchasers, media, public opinion and even psychiatrists on daytime TV chat shows all clamour for counselling's head. The emphasis is on effectiveness. Can counselling abate problematic behaviour or is it just a middle class indulgence trading on Woody Allen-esque neuroses? Are counsellors professional healers or professional conversationalists? This is an important question for treatment philosophy and the practice and delivery of services. Emerging social policy presses these issues to the fore and cannot be ignored, especially in drug treatment. It has prompted many counselling services to review their practice across the sector.

## Change from within

Social policy asks counsellors to shift profoundly how they consider their role. It is not simply a shift of style but a cultural shift of how they think about therapy. This has its roots in two historical shifts. In the US, the review of counselling effectiveness for the payment of Medicare insurance in the late 1970s demanded more stringent evidence that treatment was not only effective, but what interventions were effective for what disorders. Parallels in the NHS internal market have driven similar 'purchasing' concerns. To use evidence based practice, using clinical outcomes to determine the selection of counselling interventions and even the *manualisation* of interventions has become the increasing norm in setting clear standards of practice. Even though practices such as manualised interventions appear to produce poorer outcomes (Myers, 1986).

The second historical force has been more subtle and gone almost undetected by the counselling industry but is important for the delivery of services. This is the reality that cultural prescription of counselling has changed. Community based counselling evolved in treating middle class neurotic concerns such as depression and anxieties. These are classed as neurotic disorders as they are disproportionate reactions to life events. However, counselling services are now commissioned to treat social exclusion. People's overwhelming reactions to poverty may not be so disproportion- ate, they are embedded in a very hostile world and their resources to get out of it may be seriously curtailed through social and educational disadvantage. Freud, Rogers, Perls and the great ideologues of counselling theory, who are still the mainstay of most counselling courses today, were not working with this client group. As such a huge chasm has emerged between counselling courses and drug work practice. Drug workers studying generalised counselling courses can find it imposs- ible to square the demands of counselling practice with the reality of their day-to-day work with problematic users. The sanctity of the counselling hour has little resonance for the street crack user. It is interesting to contrast the evolution of the 12 step fellowship movement's rapid response to crises and the more familiar style of sponsor system to the highly sanitised psychotherapy models that treat addictions.

## Changes from without

Human behaviour is shaped by the cultural forces that they are immersed in. And when these forces change, so does human behaviour. This generates new concerns as well as exorcises old ones. We need only consider the demands of life in the West 400 years ago to see how these cultural forces have changed. Back then we would have lived rural lives, learned a limited range of trades and crafts from our fathers, whilst women would be bonded to the home. There may have been one church, we travelled little and bartered surplus produce for that which we could not manufac- ture ourselves. Our range of partners and life choices would be limited within a very short life expectancy. The rise in industrialisation and transportation demanded we communicated over a wider area so we needed the written word, and our time became increasingly commodified into money demanded arithmetic. As a result, education is now a necessity. As history progresses, diversification of the labour market increases the labour options. We are alienated from creation in manufactur- ing conveyer belt systems of production.

Specialised knowledge itself becomes ever more salient to the market place so that we may no longer 'produce' anything tangible. We no longer work for a craftsman but increasingly for a bureaucrat that has power over us but cannot do our job, altering the power relationships of working lives. We now have exposure not only to other churches but other religions and even the possibility of no religion at all. Our choice of life partners multiplies. Technology speeds up the pace of life and specialised knowledge becomes even more of a value commodity demanding more and more education. We can now reside in a virtual world. The victory of feminism adds the career and market place pressures of men onto women, whilst they must still remain bonded to the home. Now we can remain in education until the age of thirty and still not be ready for adult life. We would have lived our entire life cycle by this time 400 years ago. We live for three generations of our forebears. It is little wonder that the nature of human despair, mental health and feeling overwhelmed has changed with the acceleration of how we live our lives. Mental health diagnosis has proliferated in the last 100 years.

Counselling must evolve along with the populations it aims to assist if it is to stay relevant. But all too often there is a strange double standard at work in evaluating these shifts. When a new psychiatric pill comes along we call it progress, when a new counselling intervention emerges we call it faddish. However, the present economic and social pressure for counselling to show its worth with these most entrenched social problems is making new demands of therapists and therapy and will not abate. Ultimately the 'what works' agenda issues a challenge: can our psychological interventions address and overcome lifetimes of exclusion and despair?

## Choose your weapons

These social and economic pressures have generated a great deal of resistance in counselling services. What motivates this reluctance is easily apparent when the way counsellors select their interventions is reviewed. Research conducted by Norcross and Prochaska (1983) into counsellors' methods or orientation makes disappointing reading (see Table 2).

Clinical outcomes are one of the least significant factors in selecting a counselling style – surpassed by more self-centred preoccupations. While clinical experience could be argued as a form of outcomes measurement, it is very subjective. There is debate over the viability of measuring counselling outcomes. It is not exact but indicates trends in clients (see Clarkson, 1999). Orientation also appears to reflect the way counselling is taught. Purchasers' increased preoccupation with outcomes has not percolated through to counsellors' training. Most teaching establishments continue to advocate the great counselling ideologies of the 20th century without recourse to outcomes or research findings. Some ideologies are evidence led, but many contain key assumptions which match counsellors' personal values. Integrating theory and personal values may be good for the counsellor but it does not follow that it will benefit clients.

Lack of attention to these issues in the teaching of counselling has lead the European Therapy Study Institute not to recommend any courses to students. Their research demonstrates that qualified counsellors are no more effective than unqualified ones. Jeffrey Mason (1999), author of *Against Therapy*, describes his own experience as a counsellor '. . . I was trained for eight years and learned nothing. I am by no means a unique case. I was not a good therapist but I was certainly not the bottom of the barrel by any means.'

The much vaunted move towards registration would only preserve an unsatisfactory position. The culture instilled in counsellors remains potent and is a critical issue in changing orientation. Practice is deeply entangled in counsellors' sense of self. Reorientation demands that they re-evaluate themselves and their sense of meaning.

*Drug Induced*

**Table 2   Counsellors' methods or orientation**

| Influence | Mean average | Standard deviation |
| --- | --- | --- |
| Clinical experience | 4.2 | 0.7 |
| Values and personal philosophy | 3.8 | 0.9 |
| Graduate training | 3.6 | 1.0 |
| Postgraduate training | 3.4 | 1.2 |
| Life experiences | 3.3 | 1.1 |
| Internship | 3.3 | 1.1 |
| Its ability to help me understand myself | 3.0 | 1.3 |
| Type of clients I work with | 2.8 | 1.2 |
| Orientation of friends/colleagues | 2.8 | 1.1 |
| Outcome research | 2.7 | 1.2 |
| Family experiences | 2.5 | 1.2 |
| Own therapists' orientation | 2.4 | 1.4 |
| Undergraduate training | 2.2 | 1.1 |
| Accidental circumstances | 1.7 | 0.9 |

1 = no influence, 2 = weak influence, 3 = some influence, 4 = strong influence, 5 = primary influence.

So when I was asked to re-evaluate a struggling counselling service the starting point was to establish the values, ethics and concerns of the counselling team itself. Only by getting beside and examining the personal meaning of individuals' counselling orientations could we re-appraise what we were doing in terms of delivery, and what needed to be redirected.

This is a threatening prospect and research is often received as personal criticism rather than an opportunity for development. It is ironic that the counselling profession, with its implicit aspirations, seems to be inflexible and not able to change. This demanded that the counselling teams I managed had to make this shift in thinking about treatment. In the past the counsellor would simply choose their orientation and deliver it, with the best of intentions. Whether this helped clients was not the issue but was assumed. If it did not work, the client was not ready to change. Research into dependency has challenged this and undermined key assumptions, but the implications have yet to be absorbed by services.

Motivation is fostered in the relationship between client and counsellor (Miller, 1996). This questions the validity of attributing non-compliance with treatment as only the client's fault. Services become responsible for nurturing motivation. Traditionally, resolution of all stages has been attempted through application of one distinct treatment approach. The process of matching the client's personality to a treatment style was the focus of the $36 million Project MATCH, and matching achieved poor results. 'After their one-year results MATCH authors were confident only of the near futility of matching their treatment to the client attributes that they tested' (Ashton, 1999). Whilst long term figures showed better results it is important to reverse the established trend and match the treatment to the client. While counsellors allude to this, a clear framework is needed to measure each client's needs. A treatment framework exists in the substance misuse field – the Cycle of Change – which is being successfully applied to a wide range of disciplines. The research and theoretical model of Prochaska and DiClemente illustrates that dependency has an invariant series of sequential stages. The client passes through these stages and develops increased self-awareness of their drug use, problems, change and maintenance. Distinct emotions and levels of self-awareness accompany each stage (see Chapter 8).

Other established considerations must be taken into account. The quality of the counsellor's relationship with the client is central. Lambert's (1992) research estimated that 30 per cent of treatment outcomes, across all treatment styles, are driven by the interpersonal relationship. It is crucial to establish a therapeutic alliance (based on Rogers' core conditions, 1957) in the delivery of all styles (Rogers and Dymond, 1954).

In these approaches the client is the best source of solutions to deal with problems. It is essential to augment the client's opinion and self-belief that they can change. Numerous studies have shown that one of the biggest factors in clients sustaining change in behaviour and achieving goals is their positive self-belief (Marlatt and Gordon, 1985).

Unless the client takes responsibility for and ownership of any gains made they fail to nurture this insulating inner confidence in their capacity to change. The counsellor's role is to mobilise the client's inner resources rather than play the role of the expert. This involves a power shift for the counsellor, who must surrender something of their expertness. Thus, the determining role of counselling is to move people towards autonomy, not more therapy. Taking into account extra-therapeutic considerations is also very important. It is essential to help the clients establish their own support structure, which augments the therapeutic process and eventually supersedes it. Lambert (1992) suggests 40 per cent of outcomes are extra-therapeutic. These gains are achieved by the client relocating themselves back into the social institutions of life such as work, family and pro-social relationships.

## Time for change

Another consideration is time. Traditionally counselling and psychotherapy is assumed to be long term. The introduction of time limits challenges this assumption and causes consternation in the counselling classes. In many ways the length of counselling is a conflict between counsellor and client. Counsellors prefer a longer relationship, but clients do not necessarily share this view. Research by Pekarik and Finney-Owen (1987) suggests that counsellors estimate three-times the sessions necessary to resolve issues than the client did. There is a suspicion that the move to short term therapy is purely economic. To a degree it is, but on limited budgets do we offer a minority a Rolls Royce service and the majority nothing? Gains made by aiming counselling more accurately free up resources for others to receive counselling.

The duration and pace of treatment for addiction are also significant. Therapy should always begin by exploring situational factors and move into deeper areas with the client's readiness. Overprescription of treatment can have a contraindicative effect (Miller and Rollnick, 1991). At best this can promote early drop-out from treatment but at worse it can exacerbate the client's problems.

But the assumption that clients need long term therapy contains a more systematic error. On average clients only attend counselling for an average of three to four sessions. In drug services, getting a client to attend three sessions is an achievement. Counsellors should focus on what can be achieved in the sessions the client is likely to attend. While some believe this promotes symptom amelioration, it should be remembered that this light therapy is what many clients want (Lazurus, 1990). Assumptions of counselling ideology can push the counsellor to engage in work at a deeper level, not necessarily the client. Over-perfection in the counsellor can have major negative effects (Malan, 1963).

It is generally felt that short term counselling is not effective but research studies dispute this – specifically in counselling (Talmon, 1990) and addictions. Research by Edwards et al. (1977) compared problematic drinkers in intensive treatment with those who received just one advice session. Both did equally well. Barkham's (1990) research into the therapeutic curve effect indicates that the vast majority of gains are made in the first 13 counselling sessions. The therapeutic curve effect strongly indicates that over 62 per cent of treatment gains are made in the first 13 sessions, with gains drifting off dramatically over time after this (Feltham, 1998). There may be more wisdom in the 12 step adage prescribing 90 meetings in 90 days for relapsed members of the fellowship, again this corresponds with 12 weeks. This is interesting to compare to natural relationships. Clinical studies note that within human relationships disclosure rates diminish after 12 weeks of intimate contact (Argyle, 1994). Professor of social psychology John Davies (1993), who specialises in the disclosure of drug users, has highlighted a similar phenomenon. His research in drug using and non-using populations identified a high disclosure rate of up to 10 life events at the initial interview, but at three monthly follow-ups incidence decreased. Disclosure rates followed a persistent pattern across two years, with the number of events rising from one for the month after the last interview to three for the month prior to the next interview. This might suggest that the initial core concerns which drive people to enter counselling are subsumed over time by less dramatic concerns. In longer term counselling it is all too easy for clients to use sessions merely to observe the general traffic of their lives, having wrestled out the pertinent issues.

## Long time running

Progress is very slow after this, culminating over a two year period. This certainly equates with both Levinson's (1986) and Marcia's (1987) life course studies, which suggested that significant change in life course took approximately two years to build up to crises and two years to settle into a new order. The most recent evidence comes from the Project MATCH study of interventions in alcoholism. There were no statistically significant outcome differences between the three treatment modalities. But the motivational interview programme achieved its results in three to four sessions, as opposed to the 24 '12 step' sessions or 12 CBT sessions.

Very brief therapies – one session approaches – show robust findings for alcohol treatment, such evidence is scant for drug dependency at present (Drummond and Ashton, 1999). The fact alcoholism is a later onset as a condition for the majority may explain this. Early onset drinking is as intractable as early onset drug use because the experience precludes individuals from gaining any skills and preparedness for life. Later onset alcoholics will often have had successful careers, relationship and cultural connection, prior to the later onset problems. Hence whilst they may consume more, they have more skills to meet the cultural demands of life.

Many clients come to services in crisis, which elicits fast tracking to intensive treatment services. These often fail because individuals feel pushed into taking action without first having looked at the costs and benefits. Unless they are given adequate time to process and prepare for change, they may experience post-decisional regret which undermines future progress. The findings of the National Treatment Outcomes Study which is assessing the effectiveness of British drug treatment services, support the general thrust of transtheoretical approaches (Ashton, 1999). Whilst service quality is patchy and relapse rates remain high across all services, the effects of treatment do appear to be cumulative. Even if individuals do not complete treatment, they do not return to previous levels of use.

As a result, when developing counselling services for an agency we considered six sessions to be optimum, then a one-month break and a review. Sessions do not have to be weekly but can be negotiated to offer support for longer. This indicates to clients that they are not sufficiently dysfunctional to need professional support to cope. The review explores gains and how the client has progressed since counselling. Again, the central focus is on autonomy. If there are unresolved issues or goals, further contact can be agreed. We cannot assume that long term counselling is for everyone, but neither can we assume that short term counselling is. Extra sessions must be for clear therapeutic reasons. If counselling is terminated there is always a way back to the service if the necessity arises. This provides back-up but does not hijack the client's self-worth.

## Treatment no-man's land

Before reviewing counselling services, this arm of treatment was often a ghetto for clients who did not like group work, were not ready for rehab or were deeply ambivalent. Limiting direct self-referral, clients were referred by internal and external services which have prepared the groundwork. On entering counselling, clients had already established clear goals that allowed counsellors to focus on the counselling – maximising the experience. Alongside, we developed the KICK service (Krises Intervention Counselling and Keyworking). Clients not in contact with services go to a one-hour KICK session, which can be extended up to three sessions. Clients who want advice, to resolve ambivalence, or need support for a short time can get appointments quickly. They need not have counselling, but can be referred if appropriate. KICK establishes goals and supports clients to find the best treatment path, rather than beginning therapeutic work itself.

To implement the review consultation with the counselling team was essential. As was training and supervision to give them the skills necessary to deliver the service. To promote consistency, issues are shared and discussed at regular counselling allocation meetings. Implementation and success of this review is largely due to the personalities and attitudes of the counselling team, who remain open to development suggestions. The first six-monthly figures since the review have come through and we see marked improvements in attendance, outcome and throughput rates. KICK referrals to internal services show high compliance rates. And the service now provides a central plank of admission into more carefully planned and considered treatment.

## Conclusion

The review and restructuring of these counselling services has not been without detractors. A counsellor questioned my counselling ethics because of this review. It was as if the delivery of a more effective service should be subservient to preserving unquestionable counselling ideologies. I was reminded of the Rosenhan's (1973) experiment in the 1970s. Eight sane people admitted themselves to mental health hospitals in the US, reporting hearing voices. Once admitted they behaved normally, to see how long it would take to be discharged. Medical staff discharged none as sane, yet other patients realised these individuals had no illness. The staff interpreted these pseudo-patients' behaviour in accordance with an established medical ideology. What did not fit was discounted. This inability to separate reality from the means that we have of reading it is not limited to the mental health profession but is an innately human error. Treatment ideologies are necessary to guide counsellors, but can blinker and limit. Challenging research findings can remind us to keep in touch with reality. No ideology should save us the effort of thinking, just as no treatment philosophy should save clients from restoring the dignity of their lives.

Throughout the review it was important to remember that we were not championing one counselling system over another. As research continues it is essential that counsellors allow themselves to be enriched by it – to maintain a spirit of openness and learning, which will evolve as research does. The 'die rather than change' approach to therapy, and resistance to facing challenging research, erodes counselling's integrity. Wherever counselling's validation might be, it is certainly not in the past. Newly emergent treatment interventions are leading the way, not just in understanding addiction but in our whole understanding of human change itself and as we shall see, have placed addiction work at the very cutting edge of psychology.

Adapted from 'Concrete Counselling', *Druglink* 2000, 16 (1)

# Chapter 10

# Ignition of Change

*I have myself seen these sad events, and played no small part in them.*

Virgil

Miller and Rollnick's (1991) *Motivational Interviewing; Preparing People to Change Addictive Behaviour*, met the dictum of a true classic. Everyone bought it but few actually read it. Undoubtedly one of the most influential titles in recent years, the book has now reached its 2nd edition. It also provides an interesting insight into the evolution of the core ideas and research of this intervention. Immediately one notices that it carries a different sub-title, *Motivational Interviewing: Preparing People for Change* (Miller and Rollnick, 2002). This marks an important ideological shift. The 2nd edition focuses on the issue of how do *people* change rather than substance misusers change, as if they were a breed apart from humanity. Whilst the nature of human problems may be diverse, the human processes of change and adaptation seem common across present populations. As a result motivational interviewing's influence has percolated wider health domains of areas such as mental health, patient-medication compliance and exercise regimes and offending behaviour. The authors have moved closer to Prochaska and DiClemete's (see Chapter 8) research on intentional change as an attitude towards one's problems, rather than minutia of specific 'disorders' themselves. And that these attitudes shift in levels of awareness and readiness to change. It also debunks the assumption of the unique addiction psychopathology which the authors lament has led to abusive and inhumane practice in the field.

As Miller (1996) recounts, traditionally, it was believed that motivation was a kind of personality fault common to people who were dependent. Those who came forward to ask for help were motivated whilst those who did not, or dropped out of treatment centres, were seen as not being motivated enough. Many people believed, and some still do, that the drug user had to reach a traumatic crisis in their life before they realised the damage their dependency was inflicting on themselves and others. This was referred to as reaching 'rock bottom'. Only when rock bottom was reached would they finally come forward and admit that they had a problem which needed addressing.

More recent research has demonstrated that these approaches, and the assumptions that underlie them, are misguided. Study revealed that the prevalence of traits such as denial, rationalisation and projection are not endemic amongst drug or

*Drug Induced*

alcohol users (Miller, 1996). No more so than any given group of people from society, users or not. And if anything, confrontational approaches are likely to be the least effective way of sustaining long term change in people (Miller, 1998).

It had also been recognised that some people did not need to reach rock bottom before they turned their lives around. These people were referred to as 'high bottom' users. People became interested in what helped these people turn their lives around. One common influence appeared to be the people around them. Those who offered support in the shape of friends, family and work colleagues. Another question then arose. Would it be possible to raise the 'bottom' for other dependant people so that they could make changes before they reached a total crisis point (Miller 1996)?

It would be very difficult to track down the significant others in drug users' lives to find out what support they gave that was so effective. Instead studies were being done on the personalities of counsellors and the influence that these had on helping people who were drug dependent. What emerged was interesting and surprising.

People's motivations for change varied dramatically from therapist to therapist. And negative outcomes appeared directly proportional to the degree of confrontation expressed by the therapist (Miller, 1996). The greater the conflict the worse the outcomes. This has given rise to a new conceptualisation of motivation. It is not a property of personality but the product of certain kinds of relationship. These relationships are characterised by empathy, optimism, allowing individuals to maintain responsibility for their decisions and offering clear, but non-judgemental, feedback to inform this decision making. Just as addiction exists in the breakdown in wider pro-social relationships, treatment germinates with the reinitiating of pro-social relationships.

## Necessary but not sufficient

Miller and Rollnick also place renewed emphasis on motivational interviewing as a natural development of Carl Rogers (1957) person centred approach. Certainly the core conditions of empathy, positive regard, congruence and warmth remain central to its effective delivery. This is supported by a plethora of consistent research findings (Lambert, 1992; Luborsky et al., 1993; Bordin, 1976). Taking this further, the authors borrow Rogers rather unquantifiable phrase, describing motivational interviewing as 'a way of being' with the client. Certainly the vagaries of Rogers' description of the core conditions and his insistence that they are unteachable, allows many therapists to project their own interpretations upon this with little criteria for correction. This malleability may explain some of Rogers' mass appeal as essentially a blank slate for therapists' personal values.

For Miller and Rollnick, this 'way' is characterised by the deep focusing technique of reflective listening. Core to the interaction, reflective listening retains its 'advanced empathy' flavour, which both paraphrases the client and fishes beyond into the unsaid meaning at the same time. As such it searches beneath the client's answers without intruding upon them, evoking the un-stated meanings and undercurrents of the client's presentation. As such it differs from classic empathetic listening where open questions are deployed to build a picture of the client's problems, which is made clear to them through the process of making it clear to the therapist. Instead reflective listening searches for the meaning beneath the meaning, and so unravels the thread of their thinking to elicit the deeper concerns that are often missed. As such, it is a seductive listening style that seeps deep into the client's concerns. Its focused, applied listening demands accuracy which is a major contributor to treatment outcome (Crits-Christoph et al., 1993). Its nature, function and application has been much expanded, to a point that 'without which motivational interviewing cannot be practised' (Miller and Rollnick, 2002). Certainly the organisation of the 1st edition of *Motivational Interviewing* gave the impression of a cluster of techniques to be deployed pre- and post-decision making. Sharing Rogers apparent distrust of micro-skills in favour of authenticity, motivational interviewing has since matured into a more integrated approach, underpinned by the reflective listening technique. Whilst generating greater coherency, the allusion to Rogers also provides some camouflage for the ethical concerns (Miller, 1994) and a profusion of micro-skills alike.

## Universal context

The authors reiterate MI is specifically aimed at initiating the treatment process. And Prochaska and DiClemente's research has clearly shown that different therapeutic strategies are necessary for different stages of change. Motivational interviewing is a universal application for those contemplating change. It is not the panacea for all ills at all times as hailed as by its more fundamentalist supporters. The approach may spark natural remission in some clients. Miller and Rollnick's (2002) research identified that this can be the case with alcohol users but not drug users. Again, this is likely due to the early onset of drug addiction which is precluding people from developing the skills necessary for adult life, whilst alcoholism tends to manifest itself as a breakdown within adult life. As such, motivational interviewing may help alcoholics to get back on track but drug users must enter into a deeper process of learning the skills for adult life.

This context is especially important as motivational interviewing is not a counselling style in a traditional sense. Its primary aim is to facilitate a decision regarding change and fortify the client's confidence in enacting it. As such it is the framework where treatment can be decided, not necessarily the treatment in itself. Certainly we know from research that not every approach works for every person (McMurran, 1997) and the more choice that we feel we have the more in control we feel (Miller and Rollnick, 2002). For some clients this may be an institutional treatment pathway, but for others it may be more idiosyncratic. Indeed, where motivational interviewing shows its most robust outcomes for drug users is as a primer for people entering into treatment services, who show far higher levels of retention and completion after receiving this initial intervention. As such, motivational interviewing has an egalitarian vision of other treatment models. The relevancy of any treatment path must be determined by the client, not the counsellor. Adaptations do exist which present structured treatment models, notably Community Reinforcement (see Meyers et al., 1998; Smith et al., 2001; Regan et al., 1999; Abbot et al., 1998). This emergent variation is absent in the 2nd edition, which retains its focus on the brief intervention strategy to allow the client to self-elect these personalised treatment paths.

## The crucible of change

As an intervention, motivational interviewing retains its focus on the two predominant forces in the contemplator's struggle: ambivalence and anxiety. As the authors (1991) emphasised in the 1st edition 'Ambivalence is the problem'. A term defined by Bleuler (1950), ambivalence describes the presence of contradictory emotions in one person towards the same object. It is a damned if you do, damned if don't experience, which paralyses the process of change. For the problematic user, considering change is not merely limited to the absence of intoxication in life, it is the absence of one's current life, however desolate, for some unknown future. This decision has wide ranging implications which need to be fully understood, and inevitably elicits mixed emotions. Critically wider research bears this out. Prochaska et al. (1994) identified resolution of ambivalence in contemplation as the central factor in promoting change by uncovering the only laws of behavioural change to be found. The strong principle of change states that we must increase the client's awareness regarding the pros of change first and then the cons. Within this we must have twice as many pros as cons for change to occur. Where clients fall short on this ratio, further consciousness raising is needed to shift this balance. For the heavy user, this entails accepting the positive, functional role a substance has in their life whilst recognising the increasingly negative consequences too. Again these must be their own benefits and their own concerns.

It is managing this ambivalence in the pre-decision making stage (Phase 1) where motivational interviewing has developed itself the most. The 1st edition highlighted the importance of exploring both positive and negative aspects of ambivalence through the use of decisional balance sheets. Here every pro, then con, is systematically catalogued. This was followed up by the use of more directive approaches which were culled from other areas of psychology.

Developments in motivational interviewing now fuse other processes with the ambivalence mapping. Building on key determinants of opinion forming, it was recognised that when the sense of self is threatened, people engage in defence behaviours and distortion of self-presentation. Rogers (2000) had recognised this process and labelled it sub-ception meaning 'below perception'. This was elucidated more deeply by Brehm and Brehm (1981) in their theory of reactance. Under these conditions a reactance occurs where we tend to form opinions in contradiction to that which threatens us and militate arguments to exonerate ourselves. Secondly, these arguments do not reside ready made within ourselves. Only when we hear ourselves speak our opinions do they fossilise into our received view of the world. Thus confrontation has the reverse effect on change, embedding people in contrary opinions which protect their sense of vulnerability. Reflective listening, developing the client's own stated concerns, bypasses the need for the therapist to highlight problems and instead seduces the client to hear themselves speak about problems. This increases the gravitas of their concerns, which as we have seen, may include issues of health, mortality, or the continued breakdown of their functioning through external pressures.

Thus 'change talk', manoeuvring the client to hear themselves speak about the need to change, augments commitment to the process. Indeed, careful analysis into effective motivation interviewing now shows a far higher ratio of client to therapist talk. This is a delicate balancing act in practice and can only be achieved by indirect means of reflective listening. Motivational interviewing is highly reliant on the assumption that the stated attitude-behaviour link is a potent reinforcer of change. This is to say people are more likely to follow through on behaviours which are consistent with their stated values. However, some research has shown this to be more tenuous (see Hogg and Vaughan, 1998).

As such the apparent neutrality of the therapist remains key in this process, advocating no position lest they tilt the client the opposite way. Ambivalence is accepted as normal and signals of resistance are important feedback to the counsellor about their own style. Exploration of both sides of the ambivalence is critical and needs to be held carefully lest the client is tilted by the counsellor's ambitions. For example, the authors recognised that even using the conjunctive 'but' when the counsellor summed up the pros and cons has the effect of overruling what proceeded it. Whereas 'and' balances the pros and the cons without favour.

## Uncomfortable lightness of being

Once ambivalence is explored and the client manoeuvred into speaking more deeply about their own concerns, the therapist now asks the client to consider what is important in their life. What are their values, goals and aspirations? This is the engine of motivation. Remaining neutral, the therapist then invites the client to contrast these personal values in relation to the stated pros and cons of change and to consider in which capacity are these aspirations more likely to be fulfilled. With change or stasis? It is within this process of contrasting stated goals with actual behaviour that builds on the second force in the contemplator's struggle: dissonance.

Initially this juxtaposition was a distinct technique. But now the 2nd edition merges it directly to the stated feelings of ambivalence. This creates a deeper state of discrepancy in the client, where personal values can appear manifestly incompatible with their chosen lifestyle. It is this discrepancy which initiates a deep level of stress in the individual called cognitive dissonance. Owing much to Festinger's (1957) research, cognitive dissonance is a state of anxiety which is so potent it can be measured across the skin and persists for up to two weeks (Draycott and Dabbs, 1998 ). To regain psychological equilibrium, the client must either change behaviours or use more drugs to alleviate the uncomfortable realisations (Miller, 1996). Which strategy they adopt is determined by their self-belief in their capacity to manage change. Whilst the 2nd edition gives more attention to developing confidence in change, it does not fully build upon research from Bandura (1969; 1997) from which it is drawn.

Several anxiety surfacing approaches are described in the 2nd edition. These include the client hearing themselves talking about the need for change, directly asking about 'worst' fears and reverse psychology techniques such as suggesting they are not ready for change yet, which plays upon the theory of reactance. Such applications have drawn criticism as being manipulative (Miller, 1994). The 2nd edition tries to disguise them, even claiming that use of dissonance is not drawn from Festinger's work. This occurs when discussing *consonance*, the togetherness of client and therapist, adding some confusion to his obvious influence throughout the book.

Certainly, in teaching motivational interviewing, many practitioners are troubled by the amplification of anxiety. It cuts across the liberal humanistic culture of psychotherapy. In the 2nd edition, the apologetic tone, additional chapter on Ethics and continued reference to Rogers does little to disguise the consequences of deploying these stratagems. As a culture we have a desire to sedate crises with drugs or mollify them through counselling, as if they served no other purpose in the human psyche but to cause unnecessary discomfort. But as we have seen in the review of life journey, the crisis moment has a great therapeutic value in change. It is as if sufficiently powerful forces are necessary to break the bonds of our current embeddedness, and liberate us to re-embedding in more fulfilling ones. Only through disequilibrium is this possible.

Reviewing addiction therapy we see that all styles of approach centre on the management or creation of anxiety. From the boot camps to tough love. Rock bottom is a crisis point of realisation driven by anxiety. And the traditional confrontation of denial aims to remove the insulation from the consequences of problematic use, again liberating anxiety. In motivational interviewing, dissonance can only be induced where a contradiction already exists between behaviours and stated goals. This contradiction cannot be created, only surfaced. It is not used as a tool to dupe people nor is it a counsellor championing a position. It is a confrontation between the client and their most uncompromising adversary; themselves. Further-more, raising these concerns with the client now, alerts them to the possibility of a deepening crisis in the near future. In essence, the 'rock bottom' is brought forward in the client's consciousness without them having to experience it. Instead they have the opportunity to avert it.

## Miracle workers

Retaining the trappings of the 1st edition, Phase 2 has undergone a dramatic realignment. Once the decision to change is made, Phase 2 borrows heavily from solution focused therapy (see Walter and Peller, 1992). The approaches share a collaborative ideology, best characterised by DeShazer's (1995) maxim, 'If the therapist's goals and the client's goals are different, the therapist is wrong'. Asking the client to envisage perfect hypothetical solutions to establish goals, solution focused therapy assists in creating a vision of an alternative lifestyle where the individual's personal values and aspirations can be expressed. Again, this is not prescriptive but determined by the client and solution focused therapy provides the framework where this can be developed.

As such it is a more apposite intervention for those entering the preparation stage of change. Solution focused work also has the additional advantage of a more systematic homework structure. This is vital post-decision making. The early strategies of change focus on thought processes such as developing awareness, decision making and planning. The latter stages are based on action and implementation. Homework tasks can provide an important bridge to phasing in this shift, though directing tasks outside the therapeutic consulting room has traditionally been seen as an anathema in traditional counselling approaches (see Rosenthal, 2000). Solution focused therapy's emphasis on 'doing' outside the therapy session is vital, as mastery of experience remains the most potent source of self-belief (Bandura, 1997). This is underscored by the fact that the weakness inherent in most skills based counselling interventions do not ship out well into real life, where low confidence and competing sub-goals can so often conspire against the most well intended strategies. Certainly, solution focused therapy hopes to minimise the internalised stresses incumbent in the preparation stage of change (see Chapter 8) by iterating that tasks do not have to be a success, but instead begin to use such experiences to build increasing confidence.

## Conclusion

MI is a thief in the temple of 'what works'. It remains highly derivative of key developments in psychology and is not always courteous to the contribution of its sources. Yet the authors have developed the intervention into a more unified structure, and continue to capitalise on significant research drawn from their own trials and related fields. The 2nd edition does have an honesty which subverts the hype MI has generated. The new chapter on its efficacy states clearly that there are 'no studies addressing the efficacy of motivational interviewing in a relativity pure form'. Whilst it describes promising though inconstant findings, the authors remain loyal to a spirit of continued refinement and systematic scrutiny. This is in an age where too much psychotherapy still resembles Edwardian politeness and traditional addiction treatment remains obliged to a pre-war morality. Therapy must reflect the needs of both the individuals and the cultures it aims to treat. MI remains at the vanguard of that venture.

Based on an article 'Motivate Anew', *Addiction Today*. November 2002

# Chapter 11

# The Bi-Cycle of Change: A New Perspective for Treatment of Dual Diagnosis

*Canst thou not minister to a mind diseas'd*
*Pluck from the memory a rooted sorrow,*
*Raze out the written troubles of the brain,*
*And with some sweet oblivious antidote*
*Cleanse the stuff'd bosom of that perilous stuff*
*Which weighs upon the heart.*

William Shakespeare

Dual diagnosis has become a critical issue for both drug and mental health services. The complexity of problems experienced by clients belies the simplicity of the classification of merely the co-existences of problematic substance use alongside a mental health problem. Indeed, we must first expand mental health to also incorporate wider social functioning in both personality disorder and learning disability. One only has to consider the legions of permutations of possible chemical and behavioural dependencies that could partner an equally diverse range of mental health disorders to comprehend the challenge that dual diagnosis presents to treatment services. Include personality disorders, learning disabilities, poly drug use, multiple mental health disorders and degrees of severity into the equation and we soon discover that the label 'dual diagnosis' is not adequate to contain such a huge spectrum of interlocked need. The infinite range of vectored problems can be overwhelming for the practitioner, whose first inclination may be to refer on, leaving the client in a state of perpetual motion from one service to another.

A depressed businessman with an alcohol problem, a homeless person diagnosed with schizophrenia using crack on the streets or an individual with a mild learning disability living in a socially impoverished but independent environment smoking cannabis will all present very differently. We may also observe a distinction in the primary and secondary diagnosis. Individuals whose mental health problems precede use tend to be less well established in drug using networks, and as a result only have access to a limited range of easily available substances such as alcohol and cannabis. Whereas those whose mental health issues originate from their substance use, tend to be more deeply embedded in a social network that grants them access to a wider spectrum of substances and more chaotic using patterns.

## Population specifics

Within dual diagnosis it may be apt to separate the 'constants' from the 'variable' aspects of these disorders before outlining the detail of treatment. The constant aspects may be considered as the enduring mental health problems, personality disorder or learning disability that the individual may not freely choose to change, whereas the variable aspects may be those addictions and behaviours the client can choose to change. These constants may have specific impacts on the development of substance misuse problems, amplify the consequences of use and limit any attempt to resolve them through 'insight' based talking cures.

Mental health disorders may vary widely in their degree, duration and reoccurrence. Neurotic disorders, typified by a disproportionate reaction to life events, such as depression or anxiety, tend to be episodic. Whereas psychotic disorders, where the individual no longer shares a common reality with others, is considered more debilitating and enduring as in schizophrenia or bipolar depressions. Both orders of mental health disrupt social functioning leaving individuals isolated, whilst at the same time disrupting thought processes. This may amplify a substance positive reinforcing effect, as the only perceived enriching experience available to them in an increasingly unmanageable world. At the same time, it may provide a totem of identity that ingratiates them in the more permissive and accepting social world of drug using. However, the disruption in thinking may lead them to attribute substance related problems to other causes rather than high consumption. For example, the delusional individual may see it as evidence of a conspiracy, whilst the depressed individual may construe problems as symptomatic of the hopelessness that engulfs them. As a result, overtly positive expectations of the drug are not revised, which would otherwise moderate consumption. And the higher anxiety generated may reinforce the expectations that the drug will alleviate stresses and symptoms, fuelling even greater consumptions.

Personality disorders vary from mental health problems in that they are seen as a facet of the individual personality. As such they are considered enduring with a poor responsiveness to treatment of any kind. Their defining feature is that they are ego-syntonic. The individual is unable to accept responsibility for events or situations that they find themselves in, and difficulties are universally attributed to the others, not themselves (Elkin, 1999). In short, they have no ability to self-reflect on their own behaviour. As such, they will often experience the same problems repeatedly in their lives, learning nothing from the experience as it is not of their making. The consequences to self, or others, through high consumption are never caused by them. Again this can lead to high levels of social exclusion and the inability to maintain intimate relationships. This means that even though some personality disorders are characterised by high social functioning and only episodic crises, the ability to reflect on self-injurious behaviour is negated. High drug and alcohol use may therefore remain uncorrected.

Within the context of learning disabilities, the autonomous behaviour necessary to physically enter drug markets, along with the necessary grammatical skills to conceptualise use and negotiate procurement, limits high consumption to the mild learning disorder range. These clients do have higher self-awareness, but it is often artificially limited not by any incumbent cognitive impairment but by social impairment. The high degree of social exclusion that dominates their lives insulates them from the harsh realities but not the expectations of cultural life. The deep expectation that chemicals induce positive mood states can be understood in very concrete terms, as well as representing the trappings of being 'like others'. At the same time, being raised in highly supervised environments where intoxicants are wholly absent deprives these clients of any prior learning which might be applied to the self-directed using experience.

What these three groups share, and what may be compounded by the co-existence of all these constants in one individual, is that they all experience social exclusion. They dwell on the margins of cultural life prior to consumption, usually with poor or weakening attachments to the social institutions we can take for granted. As such, if we are to see addiction as the erosion of all relationships in pursuit of one source of satisfaction, even low consumption may be sufficient to break these frail bonds. This may lead to the rapid engulfment in problematic using lifestyles, increasing the necessity of the variable aspect of higher use. Furthermore, low expectation and a history of exclusion makes change even more remote.

## Intentional change

To develop an effective treatment framework for dual diagnosis it is essential to see beyond the presenting detail of the problems and grasp the core structure of the problem. As we have seen in Chapter 8, when working with any disorder we must remember we will never deal with it directly, we only work with the clients' attitudes to their problems, and these attitudes tend to move through invariant stages of awareness as described by Prochaska and DiClemente. Thus clients are never considered resistant to change, but reside in varying stages of readiness. Whilst this is not the only change model available, research has established a high degree of reliability in assessing and predicting change for addiction, eating, exercise and most significantly, mental health including personality disorders (Prochaska and DiClemente, 1992). However, we must remain cautious that self-insight based talking cures may have limited effect in some conditions. This may also apply at a physiological level in organic brain disorders such as alcohol dementia, where the capacity for self-awareness is diminished; or when working with the ego-syntonic personality disorder.

It is important that we make a separation between the course of the illness and the process of change. This stage model for mental health is key. The cycle of change identifies the clients' conscious attitude towards the problematic behaviours. Unless clients develop self-awareness about the nature of their problems they will not engage in treatment at any level. We may re-frame the cycle of change for mental health as a process. The client enters the cycle in early onset as a personality in disintegration without self-awareness (pre-contemplation). Under increasing incapacity to function this personality then goes into crisis where self-awareness increases (contemplation). This is followed by treatment engagement (preparation is often cut short through coerced treatment) where a therapeutic threshold of medication is established and complied with. The personality is then stabilised (maintenance) until the episode abates or treatment breaks down (relapse). (See Figure 1.)

The stage model may be antithetical to treatment practice in medical/mental health settings, where interventions are sudden and often intrusive as in the case of

## Figure 1  The bi-cycle of change in dual diagnosis

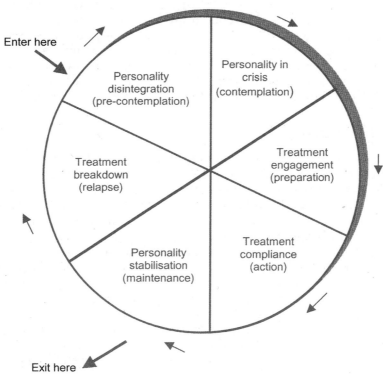

medications or surgeries. We are demanding that clients enter into and appreciate active sustained behaviour change as important, before developing awareness of the problems. However, as many clients from these sub-groups may have dislocated awareness of the problem, it may remain increasingly unimportant to them and they may be liable to react against such enforced change. At the same time, staff who perceive drug use as the problematic may experience this client group as hostile and ungrateful. This leads to a breakdown in the relationships, compromising any opportunity for therapeutic gain. Short cuts often end in failure.

## Twin processes

Considering this stage model it becomes apparent that the varying levels of client self-awareness demands very different treatment approaches. Clear assessment of the client's position in the cycle allows services to then 'match' the most effective treatment response for clients in that particular stage. As we have seen, initiating change demands very different skills to sustaining these changes. Treatment services tend to provide a 'one size fits all' approach to provision or intervention. This may meet some but not all need. The onus is on services to either provide a spectrum of corresponding treatment responses or for therapists to recognise their skills and limitations in working in each stage. Likewise, tailored psychosocial treatments for specific mental health disorders, such as managing hearing voices or anxiety control, are only usefully delivered for clients in stabilisation. A framework which allows us to dovetail effective treatment responses appropriate to the client's mental health and dependency is needed.

Whilst this matching process is important in treatment, dual diagnosis represents a more complex problem than merely identifying and providing appropriate drug and mental health treatments in concert. Whilst the NHS guidance (Department of Health Report, 27767) has recognised that change processes are incremental in the dually diagnosed, through the adoption of the Osher and Kofoed model, this is not without limitation. Osher and Kofoed (1989) reveal the importance of key treatment stages of engagement, persuasion, treatment and relapse and the need to match intervention to each stage. However research into change highlights a critical theme. Our self-confidence and expectancies in our ability to change, and the strongest predictors of treatment outcomes, are not global but specific (Bandura, 1997). Our self-belief in our ability to drive is not the same as our self-belief in our performance at maths. A dual diagnosis client's confidence to adjust to constants, or change variables are not inextricably bound together but can be seen as two independent concerns, with varying degrees of confidence, motivation and expectations about changing each domain. Essentially dual diagnosis clients are moving through a dual process of self-awareness, one regarding drug use, and the second regarding the constant, be it mental health, personality disorder or learning disability.

The most problematic area for treatment thus occurs when lag exists between these two processes. Clients may present to mental health services as a personality in crisis but be pre-contemplative about changing their drug usage. Alternatively, they may present for drug treatment in contemplation but be unaware of their personality in disintegration. I would suggest this is essentially a lag of one stage back. A client diagnosed with schizophrenia will make little progress through the mental health stages whilst they remained pre-contemplative about their crack use for instance. Unless these forces can be corralled into harmony, progress will be halted.

## The rock and the hard place

Essentially this creates a deep ambivalence in clients who have contradictory feelings towards changing. Gridlocked between a desire to use drugs versus a will to improve mental functioning (or vice versa) paralyses change and generates anxiety. In such circumstances the client has one of two choices. To opt for an anxiety reducing strategy and change problematic behaviours, or opt for a fear reducing strategy and increase drug use to suppress uncomfortable feelings (see Chapter 10). The major determinant in selecting either option is the client's belief in their capacity to manage change, and such self-belief is much diminished in people with mental health issues who may tend towards a helpless attitudinal position regarding life issues (Bandra, 1997). Particularly for those who have already acquired a case history of consistent failure, which although may be the problem of treatment mismatching, the client is likely to interpret as their failure.

This is complicated by the fact they are ambivalent in a range of treatment services that cannot accommodate this contradiction. People cannot have their baseline functioning assessed whilst chronic use masks or amplifies signs and symptoms of mental health, rendering diagnosis, and entry into mental health services impossible. Whilst drug services, vastly under-trained in mental health management, are under-confident in taking on clients with complex needs. The dual diagnosis client is therefore also locked in a situational ambivalence. Here they are offered limited access to positive reinforcement (through support) versus a powerful desire to escape the hostile situation they are in (through rejection). Falk's (1981) illuminating research on compulsivity in Chapter 3, conclusively demonstrates that when trapped between equal and opposing forces, the highest levels of compulsive behaviours are generated in humans. 'Poised between schedules of commodity availability and situational escape, the adjunctive behaviour often functions to preserve the situation.' The adjunctive behaviour becomes a displacement activity whilst negative or positive forces either abate or intensify and a clear choice can be made between fight or flight. This waiting period is the sink hole where many dual diagnosis clients remain trapped and compulsivity escalates as a result (see Chapter 8).

Practitioners must develop a skills base in squaring ambivalence in dual diagnosis clients in order to bring and keep both processes in harmony and direct the client towards simultaneous change. As we have seen in Chapter 10, motivational interviewing, with its focus on resolving ambivalence, has been found to be a highly effective treatment strategy for dual diagnosis (Carey, 1996). This may be because in practice, any shift in attitude towards change in one domain will heighten conflicts in the other domain, demanding the client face or manage concerns they feel unable to accept or manage. For example, a crack using client who was diagnosed with a psychotic disorder I key worked, moved through pre-contemplation to action in both constant and variable concerns. However, when considering what might be necessary to maintain his mental health status, and bring this into line with his abstinence of drugs, deep resistance emerged in him. Although this might be construed as the end game, what was striking was that the ambivalence remained as deep, even in this last shift. As such, working with dual diagnosis clients demands a constant vigilance for ambivalence that will emerge at every gear shift. The squaring of mixed feelings is ever necessary. It is little wonder, that in everyday practice, the dual diagnosis individuals' change process may take twice as long and demand workers are twice as sensitive.

It must also be recognised that besides the interpersonal skills needed to address psychological ambivalences there must be a change in the politics of service provision. Increasing the accessibility to services must play an integral part in tilting the balance of situational forces in favour of positive change to address situational ambivalence as well: because all the skills in the world mean nothing when the client cannot receive them.

## What and when?

Whilst relationships and ambivalence work remain perennial concerns, the treatment of dual diagnosis, the stage of change itself will demand specific responses. We need to consider what orientation the key mechanism of change must take within these client groups. Whilst employing the mechanisms to address addiction outlined in Chapter 8, we must translate these mechanism to apply to the specific populations constant in parallel to variable drug use. For example, for the pre-contemplative clients we need to raise awareness of the constant, or its effect. This is more pertinent to clients experiencing their first episode of mental health, where the personality may experience some disintegration but the client attributes their problems to the world. A deep empathy for the client's perspective, and acceptance of their reality is essential first before the gentle question arises, is it the world or how they perceive it right now? This may elicit a powerful internal reaction as the client realises their crisis is situated in them. The personality disorders egosyntonic character makes consciousness raising difficult. Close joint assessment of life history, demonstrating repeat patterns of behaviour, with them as a common denominator, may spark concern and some self-reflection. Their inclination to attribute all problems externally demands a gentle but sustained focus on the task, which may become obstructed by self-protecting diversions. Whilst individuals with mild learning disabilities are often all too aware of their life situation and the exclusions they experience as a result. Anger and frustration at their predicament is often left unrecognised and no vent is given to these feelings within many support services. Often the least trained and skilled workers are left to 'hold' these populations, in a low pay, low prestige role. However, often the mild learning disability cognitive style which tends toward being unilateral means there are not as many competing sub-goals in the individual's life, making interventions more focused and less prone to being undermined by a suffuse range of other wants. Greater enrichment through social inclusion and recognition of their wants and needs as being the equal to any other adult would do much to negate the need for them to seek out satisfactions that may only be available to them in the shadow society. Social liberation is ever salient to this group, so often ghettoised in high support but isolating services.

In this way, each mechanism can be combined to tailor treatment interventions which are specific to the particular needs, whilst reflecting the broader processes of change (for a complete overview of this treatment strategy, see Watkins et al., 2001). In my clinical experience, escorting the client across all stages is preferable. However, meaningful professional relationships for people in otherwise isolated lives can prove extremely powerful. Transference and attachment can result in treatment gains being ascribed to the therapist rather than the client's own self-regulation. We will not change anything for clients by the sheer magnitude of our concern. Our role is to provide the framework. Choices, responsibility and progress remain with the client, and must not be limited to the purely biological or psychological but must include the social arena as well.

## Conclusion

Respecting the individual's needs and concerns is of vital importance for this client group, who are often expected to remain obliged to the passive receipt of treatment. When our interventions are rejected, non-compliance is perceived as the product of the disorder and not the relevancy. Whilst we must be cautious not to sell the false hope that every life can be fully restored, we should not allow a sceptical vision pervade our encounters that a higher quality of life is impossible. People can and do make huge gains within these populations. Understanding how this can be sustained needs to be our concern, rather than bleak anticipation.

# Chapter 12

# Keep Taking the Tablets: Relapse in Dual Diagnosis

*They called me mad, and I called them mad, and damn them, they outvoted me.*
Nathanial Lee

Whilst motivational interviewing has become the recommended treatment approach for treating dually diagnosed individuals it does have limitations. Motivational interviewing is designed to amplify a client's state of readiness to change and initiate engagement. The initial anxiety that promotes change soon elapses. Deprived of drugs and alcohol as primary coping strategies the dual diagnosed client will struggle to *sustain* a change in behaviour in light of an immediate loss of identity and the continuance of life stresses that may prompt relapse. In order to break the revolving door treatment approach it is important that practitioners draw upon a wider range of interventions to assist the client's progress.

Marlatt and Gordon's (1985) systematic research has highlighted the necessity for a different treatment strategy to maintain behavioural change. Based on social learning theory, drug use is viewed as a learned habit rather than a biological compulsion. When a user confronts the risk of consumption, they may believe they have no choice but to use due to habitual expectation; lack of alternative skills in managing this situation otherwise; or low confidence in resisting. Failure to manage risk factors successfully is thus seen as a skills deficit. Research has highlighted that the critical determinants of relapse are limited and can be assigned to interpersonal as well as intrapersonal circumstances (see Table 3).

Individuals will have a varying susceptibility to this hierarchy of determinants. Generally, long term users and women are more likely to relapse for negative mood states. Whereas young people and short term users are more prone to relapse for positive reasons (Annis et al., 1996). It is reasonable to expect that the dual diagnosis individuals exhibit similar vulnerabilities to resuming use. As such, it is important to understand how, and where, they may figure in this client group in order to anticipate and reduce their impact.

## Conflict and negative mood states

The key area of lapse is personal conflict. Personal conflict combined with prolonged negative mood is the most likely factor to turn a lapse into a relapse (McMurran,

**Table 3   Determinants of relapse (Marlatt and Gordon, 1985)**

Intrapersonal determinants
(1) **Unpleasant emotions**: People use drugs to deal with difficult emotional states. These include negative feelings such as frustration, anger, loneliness, boredom, worry or depression. These feelings can arise when people feel blocked from achieving goals. It also includes feelings of guilt or the result of others making high demands of us.
(2) **Physical discomfort**: Drugs are used to ease physical pain. This includes physical states which relate to prior drug use such as withdrawal or cravings. It also relates to non-drug using physical discomfort such as illness, fatigue or injury.
(3) **Pleasant emotions**: Here drugs are used to enhance positive emotions such as feeling joy, in control or happiness.
(4) **Testing personal control**: This is the ex-user's desire to test their will power by using drugs in moderation or 'just the once'. This can be seen as an attempt to restore personal freedom in light of personal or external prohibition.
(5) **Urges**: This is where drug use is resumed through an inner temptation or deep urge to use. This may be accompanied by cravings or by finding oneself exposed to a situation where the drug is there to be taken.

Interpersonal determinants
(1) **Conflict**: This is where drug use is resumed after arguments or disagreements with other people. Often these encounters leave people in a negative emotional state such as frustrated, angry or guilty. Other times people might feel anxious, apprehensive or worry about the implications of the conflict.
(2) **Social pressure**: Drug use can start as a result of other people's drug use tempting people back into usage. This can be direct, as in being offered the drug. Or it can be indirect through the ex-user just observing others, such as an ex-drinker walking past a bar and seeing others through the window.
(3) **Pleasant times**: Drugs can be taken to enhance a pleasant occasion such as a wedding, sex or other celebrations. Although this enhances a positive mood the drug is taken as part of a more social interaction.

1997). With increasing emphasis in psychiatry on prescribing, the role and the nature of the therapeutic relationships has become significantly reduced. 'In the passage of psychoanalytically orientated psychotherapy from 50 per cent to 2.5 per cent of the graduate curriculum may be traced the decline and virtual demise of psychoanalysis within psychiatry . . . By 1990, more than 100 of the 163 residency programs for psychiatry in the United States had abandoned instruction in intensive psycho-therapy' (Shorter, 1997).

As it has been increasingly recognised that motivation for change is the product of the therapeutic relationship, it is important to reappraise current thinking on the impact of helper. Increasing attention is being focused on the therapeutic alliance, the interpersonal bond between client and the helper. It is the link that will hold people in contact with supportive services, reduce drop-out and increase the duration of the treatment episode (Onken et al., 1997, NIDA Monograph). The duration of treatment has been identified as a key factor in producing positive outcomes (Lubrorsky et al., 1985).

One early researcher, Bordin (1976), stated that the alliance needed to be established in three clear areas of the relationship. Firstly the helper and patient must agree on common goals. Secondly, they must also agree on the kind of treatment needed to achieve them. It is essential that the client knows exactly what to expect from treatment, both pharmacological and therapeutic. Most drop-outs occur very early on in treatment and could be the result of the patient being given an inadequate knowledge of what to expect and whether it was appropriate for them (Peterson et al., 1994). Thirdly, the helper and the patient must form a connection. There must be a mutual link between them that sustains the relationship. If the helper is unable, or unwilling, to share these goals with the client, the relationship will break down very quickly. This may present difficulty for some service providers who may only be offering one treatment. It is important that there is flexibility both in goals and treatment style where possible, in order to meet a diverse range of individuals' needs.

The quality of the therapeutic alliance seems critical in both the drug dependency field and mental health, particularly depression, and is a significant indictor of treatment success. Research indicates that the enthusiasm of the prescriber, particularly for a 'new' drug, enhances its efficacy (Dixon and Sweeney, 2000). Whilst Krupnick's et al. (1996) research compared alliance factors amongst those in psychosocial treatment against those who were merely prescribed, to 'give further support to how important the therapist-patient bond is in improving a patient's mental state . . . [On treating patients with drugs and no alliance] This could really impede a persons chance of getting better.' Again, it is striking that outcomes appeared dependant on the relationship rather than the medication. As we saw in the introduction, all drugs have both objective and subjective effects on the brain, whether self or medically prescribed. What may be occurring in medical prescribing is that the client experiences an internal change, but the nature of the drug action does not reveal itself to the user. If one trusts the prescriber, the patient may interpret this internal change positively; whilst if one does not trust the prescriber, it can be greeted with abject suspicion regardless of the biological action of the drug.

Sharing mutual goals is a challenge to statutory mental health settings which impose abstinence on the dual diagnosis client in order to gain access to, or be retained in, mental health services. This may contradict the goals of the client who may wish to move toward controlled use at this time. There is an assumption that the drug use is contraindicative and abstinence will abate symptoms but this is not always the case. Research indicated that only cocaine worsened psychotic symptoms in individuals whilst other drugs neither improved nor worsened the condition (Casteneda et al., 1991). Whilst this research should not be dismissed out of hand, it may only chart the expectations of the users rather than the reality of their use, as the ability to appraise the actuality of use may be debilitated in these client groups (see Chapter 11).

It does however remain striking that harm reduction is seen as an anathema for dual diagnosis clients, even though it is central policy for those without a diagnosis. It may also be a reflection of the values that mental health practitioners bring to the treatment setting, who are not acclimatised to the values and attitudes of working with drug users. Whilst the imposition of abstinence deters clients from seeking treatment it may be necessary for services to adopt a wider perspective. One model currently advocated in primary care settings is of the hierarchy of goals, where more consensus may be found between patient and treatment provider (Department of Health, 1998). Here, smaller incremental goals are established towards stabilising the drug use and lifestyle, with abstinence as the far end of the spectrum. Agreeing such goals may expose differing attitudes within the patient and practitioner, however, the effective intervention models clearly side with the patient in establishing their long term goals. On successful treatment approaches, Findings (1999), reported that an important determinant was, '. . . interventions geared to the patients own agenda and willingness to recognise their problems.'

This presents specific challenge in an involuntary treatment setting. Some have argued that the notion of involuntary treatment is likely to cause a direct therapeutic axis which opposes the possibility of alliance building. In one study, 55 per cent of patients reported that forced treatment made them now avoid treatment, whilst 47 per cent reported fear of forced treatment lead them to avoid services (Campbell and Scharaiber, 1989). The inability of worker and client to share goals leads to a significant discrepancy in the compliance to treatment. It is estimated that up to 70 per cent of clients do not take their prescribed medication (Dixon and Sweeney, 2000).

The dual diagnosis client sits awkwardly between two divergent axioms of these treatment populations. All too often the mental health patient wants the treatment but not the medication, whilst the drug user wants the medication and not the treatment. Under present conditions of non-compliance, enforced treatment orders may widen this chasm even further. One way to shift this position is to redress power dynamics in the patient-prescriber relationship. If the patient is coersed without addressing their concerns and readiness directly, the chance is the alliance is always likely to be flawed. The other great risk is that the prescriber talks to a member of the family and the patient is wholly excluded for these discussions. This will have a deeply contrary effect on the compliance rates and on treatment. Research shows that very often the patient is still able to make informed choices but they are withheld from the process. Protest is often perceived as a symptom of the illness and not the quality of the interaction taking place, and demands a power shift downwards from the clinical practitioners (Strong, 2000).

In many ways this presents a strong case for an external substance misuse treatment service supporting the mental health agency. There may be significant under-reporting of substance misuse by presenting patients who may well fear the consequences of disclosure or expulsion from treatment. Particularly as drug use within psychiatric institutions themselves is very widespread. This model has been very successful in some treatment services but there are also dangers. Unless compatibility is found between mental health and substance misuse interventions there could be contraindicative results, allowing clients to play workers off against each other and polarising the interventions.

## Alliance factors

Besides appropriateness of intervention, Prochaska and DiClemente recognised that the need for therapists to show empathy, warmth, congruence and positive regard (as identified by Carl Rogers, 2000) remains integral to the delivery of all interventions at all stages of the cycle of change. Research by Michael Lambert (1992) of the Society of Psychotherapy Research has supported this finding, showing that up to 30 per cent of treatment outcomes are driven by the quality of the relationship alone. However, empathy, warmth, congruence and positive regard are not sufficient in themselves to precipitate and sustain change. Research conducted in rehabilitation settings (Toma, 2000) found that, whilst clients preferred non-directive to directive qualities in a therapist, they found non-directiveness itself as the most unhelpful. They felt that they needed clear frameworks and direction rather than being left to work things out for themselves or being given solutions (see Table 4).

Toma's findings corroborate other research studies which suggest that there are key personal qualities for improving the alliance with people. One of the most important of these is therapeutic optimism. The helper believes that the clients can achieve their goals and wants them to succeed. Furthermore, that the helper can convey a hopeful attitude that goals are attainable and that they are working in partnership to achieve them. And, that the helper develops a liking for the client or at least some aspect of them (Maddon, 1990; Lubrorsky et al., 1993). In an age of increasingly pharmacological solutions to psychosocial problems, it is reassuring for therapists to note that the entry of a significant other into a constructive and collaborative dialogue is still what creates the biggest impact on behavioural change. And services can reorient themselves alone to improve outcomes (Daley and Zuckoff, 1999).

Once the alliance is established it is also very important to monitor it as the relationship develops. Sometimes we are unable to offer people what they want or we may inadvertently do or say something that offends the patient. It is important to be aware of ruptures in the alliance and, if it does become damaged, that we are prepared to address it. It is imperative to stay alert for changes in the patient's

*Drug Induced*

**Table 4  Personal qualities of the helper (Toma, 2000)**

| Non-directive attitudes | | | Directive attitudes | | |
|---|---|---|---|---|---|
| Honest | 61 | (81.3%) | Reassuring | 43 | (57.3%) |
| Genuine | 59 | (78.6%) | Guiding | 39 | (52.0%) |
| Listening | 54 | (72.0%) | Tough | 34 | (45.3%) |
| Understanding | 53 | (70.6%) | Challenging | 34 | (45.3%) |
| Warm | 52 | (69.3%) | Confrontative | 34 | (45.3%) |
| Sincere | 50 | (66.6%) | Directive | 27 | (36.0%) |
| Open | 49 | (65.3%) | Influential | 27 | (36.0%) |
| True | 38 | (50.6%) | Authoritative | 18 | (24.0%) |
| Accepting | 38 | (50.6%) | Intellectual | 15 | (20.0%) |
| Equal | 27 | (36.0%) | Leading | 14 | (18.6%) |
| Permitting | 19 | (25.3%) | Demanding | 12 | (16.0%) |
| Allowing | 17 | (22.6%) | Controlling | 10 | (13.3%) |
| Empathetic | 15 | (20.0%) | Persuasive | 8 | (10.6%) |
| Authentic | 14 | (18.6%) | Proposing | 7 | (9.3%) |
| Consenting | 10 | (13.3%) | Telling | 7 | (9.3%) |
| Enabling | 9 | (12.0%) | Dominant | 6 | (8.0%) |
| Non-directive | 6 | (8.0%) | Manipulative | 5 | (6.6%) |

attitude towards us, and be prepared to spend time reviewing the relationship in an open and non-defensive way to heal any rift (Foreman and Marmar, 1985; Coady, 1991).

The ability to relate to clients in this way is important for both mental health and substance misuse treatment. Often the mental health professional engages with the client from a position of authority whereby the patient's involvement is passive. Contrarily, under-confidence in working with mental health issues in counselling services may mean that fear or the counsellor's own sense of inadequacy to manage the presenting issues may interfere with the alliance building. Without such an alliance it remains unlikely that the patient will be retained in the service.

Perhaps the greatest challenge is in how the worker relates to their own agency. The research suggests that such alliance building is in fact a trickle down effect from the management to clinical staff teams. Those who feel compatible, engaged and in agreement with the ethos of their agency produced better outcomes. Similar findings were reported in the treatment of heroin users with methadone. In a time of public spending cuts, inquiries and increased emphasis on performance, this agency culture could indirectly have a detrimental effect on care.

## Pain and discomfort

The key second area of relapse is that of physical pain. The primary concern for the dual diagnosis client here should be that of the medication prescribed. The dual diagnosis patient is difficult to prescribe to. Most drug users have a more developed interest in pharmacology and concern with side effects of prescribed medication. Their own case history will give them a comparable experience of self-prescribed drugs which although problematic may have carried significantly less potent side effects. There is also a difficult moral distinction between condeming the use of self-prescribing illicit drugs and enforced prescription of state sanctioned substances. This issue of the side effects of psychiatric drugs can be deeply significant. For example, the side effects of neurolopetic drugs can be severe and permanent. In one report (Trafford General Hospital Press, 1998), 66 per cent of psychiatrists and 48 per cent of patients considered the severity of side effects the principle cause of non-compliance with treatment. In addition 48 per cent reported sexual side effects and 87 per cent of patients reported involuntary movement side effects. The result of this is a negative subjective experience that diminishes the clients' compliance.

Recently it has been reported that the prescribing of atypical neuroleptics, which have far less stringent side effects, has been limited due to financial constraints, despite the relatively low cost of these drugs (Chadda, 2000). In order to overcome these principal factors in the attrition rates there must be a more equitable approach to the provision of care to those with mental health issues, or at least consideration given to those most vulnerable to relapse. Breggin (1993) reports that the effectiveness of major tranquillisers is no greater than minor tranquillisers for the treatment of psychosis. However the profound side effects of other treatments besides neuroleptics should never be ignored but are often underestimated by clinical practitioners. The prescription of drugs to alleviate the side effects of medications, muscle relaxants and anti-anxiety drugs, may also create scope to foster dependency on these drugs. Consumption rates should be carefully monitored to check that the patient's supply is not exceeding the rate of the primary medication.

## Positive social groups

Whilst many biological explanation of drug use abound, what we can deduct from research is that drug use is an adaptive response to social, psychological and environment pressures. As we have seen in Chapter 3, it is important to recognise that drugs are a positive reinforcer only in the absence of alternatives. The social life of the individual cannot be neglected in the treatment package. Fortunately, the benefits of socialisation as key extra-therapeutic factors are beginning to be recognised, with a shift to greater user involvement in mental health services. This could be built upon with specific peer support groups for those with a dual diagnosis. I have noticed how patients in hospital environments always forge powerful alliances with each other when given the opportunity and this could be augmented. Especially powerful might be those who have recovered through mental health services, who may challenge the negative expectations that recovery is impossible or that the quality of one's life can never be improved.

Breaking the isolation may insulate people against the environment temptations and relapse of mental health issues. Positive peer support groups can have a powerful effect on stabilising behaviour (Ashton, 1999) and repressing urges and withdrawal symptoms (Peele, 1995a). It may also offer dual diagnosis individuals with social options which break from their old drug associated environments and peer groups. Recent research into schizophrenia highlights the effectiveness of simple approaches which are personality driven. Here nursing staff shared hobbies, interests and current affairs with a patient in befriending programmes. Outcomes were measured as effective as cognitive-behavioural programmes though the effect was more short lived. Coupled with this should be an inclusionist approach to integrate people with mental health problems within mainstream services wherever possible, to limit the stigmatisation that mental illness can breed.

## Positive moods and times

It is ironic that treatment success may well prove a high risk factor in itself. Once people have stabilised they may feel comfortable in resuming drug using lifestyles again. In my clinical experience, this has proved a major risk for clients who have made good progress. For the dual diagnosis patient, resuming drug use can be a symbolic ritual, they are 'normal' again and want to do normal activities within their peer groups. We must recognise that despite our best intentions, the client is unlikely to resist use, if on discharge from hospitalisation they are returned to the impoverishment of their previous lives.

Positive mood states are not often considered as a risk factor in relapse. As such patients may not anticipate its impact and adequately prepare for such situations. More consideration and education on these risk factors are important for it to be minimised. Besides increasing the patient's awareness of the risk factors, exploring what the patient feels the consequences of such actions might be is important. Over-confidence is as dangerous as low confidence. The 'confident incompetent' is much more likely to take on formidable challenges that they are simply not equipped to deal with adequately and is often the product of positive mood states.

## Insulating factors

The final challenge of the treatment is the long term sustainability of gains made through therapeutic treatment for the dually diagnosed individual. Treatments which are primarily pharmacology driven improve gains in the short term but are less effective in the long term (Annis, 1996). Bandura ascribes this phenomena to the importance of developing self-efficacy belief in the patient. 'Bandura has suggested that people's expectations of themselves have a great deal to do with their willingness to put forth effort to cope with difficulties, the amount of effort they will expend, and their persistence in the face of such obstacles' (Egan, 1998). Self-efficacy is the belief we have in our own competence to manage skills and situation. If gains made during treatment are ascribed to the impact of medication rather than self, this inner confidence is not nurtured and therefore makes change harder to sustain. Enhancing self-efficacy belief is an essential ingredient in the process of recovery and the continued long term sustainability of treatment gains.

Egan suggests that skills acquisition, feedback, modelling behaviour, encouragement and reducing anxiety about performance are core approaches to augment this process. The patient must recognise themselves as the engine of change and efficacy of treatment is due to them rather than support services or medications. Involvement in care planning will in itself engage the patient and offer greater ownership of the recovery process. When working with people who have experienced profound periods of helplessness this level of engagement takes time to cultivate. And the time factor is crucial. Lapse is part of the recovery process for many people. If people are given the opportunity to learn from this experience it may well prove the most important landmark in their recovery. And time, patience and the alliance are the platform where this learning takes place.

## Conclusion

The dual diagnosis patient represents the greatest challenge to substance misuse and psychiatric treatment services. There are serious resource issues at work, such as adequate prescribing, training, and low client/worker ratios. To support these vulnerable people towards change these services must take a deeper look at themselves and commit to a process of learning and development. This prospect feels just as threatening to us as it does to the patient in the foothills of change. In many ways the current trends in care are antithetical to this process but not all. With the arrival of assertive outreach teams, the delivery of service will not merely operate in the patients' own geographical terms but also on their own personal terms too. The break up of institution-centric approaches is an opportunity to include the patient as the central force in the healing process. This process is resource driven but practitioners can realign treatment priorities by turning cost led initiative into a patient led service. And this will be the greatest challenge of all.

Based on Dual Diagnosis: Facing the Challenge Conference, S. Glos. 1999

# Project Match or Project Mess?: Equalising Factors in the Largest Treatment Study Ever

*The 'career of the truth' may turn out to include a far greater degree of personal functioning than we might imagine, but the fact remains that in a world where people increasingly will put themselves in the hands of 'mental health professionals' it is the professionals above all who must understand that much of human personality is none of their business.*

Robert Kegan

Project MATCH represents the largest research project ever conducted, weighing in at $35 million. Its remit compared the effectiveness of 'matching' the personalities of problematic alcohol users to three different treatment approaches. These included 12 step facilitation, cognitive behavioural therapy and motivational enhancement. The carcass of its findings has now been thrown to the dogs. Despite the scraps being meagre, sweeping generalisations about treatment efficacy continually appear in print. This is overly simplistic. We cannot understand MATCH's results without exploring the context of these treatment approaches. And in doing so we can identify equalising factors which compromise the whole MATCH ethos.

## Adding it up

MATCH yielded successes across the three treatment modalities. Outcomes were so close that no statistical significance emerged, yet 12 step facilitation's slightly higher performance continues to be over sold. The huge cost of MATCH only makes it expensive, not definitive. Of the 4,481 people eligible for MATCH only 1,726 participated (Ashton, 1999). People were excluded on grounds of drug use, mental illness or involvement in the criminal justice system. Many refused to enter the programme because of the commitment it demanded. This suggests that motivated populations of alcohol users were inducted into treatment (Peele, 1998a). This varies dramatically from clinical practice where such filtering is impossible, and where criminal justice is increasingly the treatment forum for dependency. As a result, research in clinical settings contradicts MATCH's three way tie break. Meta-analyis of actual clinical treatment with wider problematic alcohol clients rate brief interventions highest, whilst 12 step performs badly (Miller et al., 1995).

## The big three

The treatment approaches were selected because of their differences (NIAAA Press Release, 1996). It is assumed that MATCH replicated them as they exist in the field. But they did not. Significant modifications were made to all treatments which distorted them dramatically. To understand this it is important to look at these treatments styles as they are delivered in treatment settings.

The oldest treatment approach is the 12 step fellowship (see Chapter 1). Addiction is described as a disease and the client must accept the label of 'addict'. They also had to recognise they were powerless to control their consumption. Only by accepting total abstinence from all psycho-active substances, observing 12 prescribed steps towards sobriety that they must rigorously work through, and remaining in lifelong treatment can an addict remain in control. It was also believed alcoholics suffered from a powerful defence mechanism of 'denial', so treatment approaches evolved a confrontational style. The wounded healers in self-help groups had to break down these barriers in order to reach the person underneath this defence mechanism (Kennard, 1998).

Cognitive behavioural treatments have their roots in cognitive psychology. Entranced by breakthroughs in artificial intelligence in the 1950s, computing became a metaphor for mind, and parallels were drawn between how computers learn and how the brain processes information (Richards, 2002). This key assumption has been developed by Albert Bandura in analysis of the appraisal we make before taking action (Evans, 1989) and these ideas have been generalised into structured relapse prevention (Marlatt and Gordon, 1985). Based on social learning theories, Bandura stipulated that before we take any action we make a 'cognitive' decision. This ability to reflect and choose actions is primarily a learned response. As human experience is a flux of events, individuals may not develop clear anticipation of the outcomes of their choices. Or they may not recognise the range of choices which are available because of habitually acting in a certain way. Cognitive behavioural programmes therefore focus on enabling people to anticipate risk situations and recognise this wider range of choices. Thoughts must turn these wider options into action. Their ability to do so relies heavily on their self-belief that they can do so. Positive expectations can enhance performance, leading to better outcomes, which in turn support future positive expectations; whilst the converse is true for negative expectations. Our greatest source of self-belief comes from personal mastery of challenges. Therefore skills acquisition and rehearsal of alternative behaviours is a core ingredient of treatment.

Motivational interviewing is the most recent treatment approach, developed in the 1980s by William Miller. He questioned whether the assumptions about addiction and treatment in traditional 12 step therapy were founded. Through comparing counsellors' caseloads he discovered that confrontational approaches, which labelled clients and imposed goals, generated high drop-out rates (see Chapter 10). Reviewing 'successful' treatment he recognised that motivation to change was not a personality flaw in denial ridden addicts, but was the product of the relationship between the client and the counsellor. Drawing upon a wide range of research into effective strategies, motivational interviewing recognises the central importance of a collaborative relationship between client and counsellor. An empathetic counsellor's role is to provide a framework that allows the clients to identify goals which are important to them, not necessarily abstinence. They do this by amplifying the client's anxiety about the need to change, resolving ambivalent feelings and developing a discrepancy between current behaviours and stated goals. The client is given responsibility for selecting the best treatment approach for themselves whilst the counsellor continues to support their self-belief that these goals can be achieved (Miller and Rollnick, 2002).

## The same only different

Whilst MATCH alludes to these general treatment styles, significant modifications were made for research purposes (see Kadden et al., 1992; Nowinski et al., 1992; Miller et al., 1992). For instance, 12 step facilitation created a new individualised counselling programme which integrated with the 12 step ethos. This counselling programme was then delivered by professional counsellors in out-patient settings. This is in stark contrast to the experience of 12 step fellowship which is either residential or informal community-based self-help groups. And many within the fellowship have come to regard the residential delivery of 12 step as a bastardised rendition, a hybrid of the model that has become fused with other treatment approaches. Whilst each community group may have its own very distinct style and evolve its own folklore regarding addiction and change (Sutherland, 2001). Such a distinction has been lost on many commentators. Schaler (1996) for example, has demanded the dismantling of all treatment models, except for 12 step, on the basis of these inconclusive outcomes. Twelve step facilitation did do marginally better than the other modalities but this was not necessarily due to its own treatment intervention. The 12 step facilitation was created as an adjunct to 12 step groups, and does not represent the then available treatment in the field. But the difference is profound.

Similar modifications were made to other treatment styles. Motivational enhancement, was modified from motivational interviewing. Motivational interviewing was designed to kick start change in 'contemplators', just one section of the cycle of change. It will not necessarily sustain change in maintenance (see Chapter 10). Other treatments designed for maintenance such as CBT are necessary, however motivation needs to be elicited in order to engage in such programmes (see Chapter 8). However, alternative treatments were denied to this MATCH group in order to reduce therapeutic interference. These approaches may well have initiated changes in this group but failed to sustain them in motivational enhancement, alternatively the maintenance orientated strategy of CBT may not have significantly compounded the commitment to change.

Another significant modification to motivational enhancement was the treatment goal of abstinence was imposed in each modality. Imposing goals is a direct contradiction of motivational interviewing, where the client must identify goals for themselves. This is negated in MATCH and introduces an artificial watermark into the research which does not exist in clinical practice. Despite this, the largest overall 'success' made across treatment was reduction of drinking which prefigured far higher than total abstinence. Within the underpinning assumption of motivational interviewing this would be considered acceptable as client driven, whilst cognitive behaviour models also prescribed controlled drinking programmes. However, within the disease model of 12 step, such reductions are not deemed possible as total sobriety is demanded lest the individual fall prey to progressive illness.

## Beyond treatment factors

Another great difference was time. The 12 step facilitation group attended 12 weeks of one-to-one counselling *and* AA group once a week. This constituted a total of 24 sessions. Cognitive behavioural therapy had 12 weekly sessions, whilst motivational enhancement consisted of four sessions over the 12 weeks. With non-attendance rates even across all treatment styles, the length of the interventions did not effect the outcomes of treatment success (Ashton,1999). This provides support for the much maligned brief intervention approaches.

## Collaborative engineering

Issues regarding attendance represent the greatest equalising effect in MATCH. Fear of high drop-out rates led to considerable efforts on preventing non-compliance. As one MATCH designer said '[On MATCH] . . . retention was given close attention because of the need for adequate statistical power, the need to expose patients to an adequate dose of study treatment, the need to retain a study sample that reflected the larger population from which it was drawn, and the need to avoid statistical problems associated with different attrition. Thus the author's research teams used a number of strategies intended to enhance retention' (Carroll, NIAAA Monograph). This attention was driven by existing research that clearly demonstrated interpretative approaches generate very high drop-out rates (Piper, 1999). Hence anticipated problems with treatment approaches under review were to be negated as if retention was not a significant performance indicator in itself. This is critical as the collaborative approach of motivational interviewing was drawn directly from research on the poor outcomes of confrontational styles such as twelve step; where clients are removed from treatment for 'lapsing', and reduced or controlled drinking is not considered acceptable, let alone a viable treatment outcome.

This led to the implementation of retention strategies across *all* treatment approaches. They drew upon Bordin's (1976) research on therapeutic alliance which highlighted clients setting goals, agreeing on tasks and emotional bond as critical factors in retention. In MATCH, measures to foster alliance included emergency sessions, responses tailored to clients' needs, recognition of varying levels of severity, the client's free 'air time' and self-selection of core topics in 12 step facilitation and cognitive behavioural approaches (see also Conners, 1997). This contrasts with treatment in the field where the therapist's interpretations, confrontation, labelling and denial are not only the norm but a primary focus in 12 step treatment, and skills acquisition can be highly prescriptive in cognitive behavioural treatment. MATCH disseminated these alliance strategies across all three modalities, though this again does not reflect practice in the field. Essentially this equalised the core advantages of motivational enhancement. It also begins to compromise the three treatments to a point that they *shared* common factors rather than differed. This is particularly salient as research findings support motivational interviewing ethos that outcomes are predominantly driven by the quality of the relationship not treatment style. In light of the generalised alliance factors cribbed from motivational interviewing, we cannot ascribe outcomes purely to treatment modality. And we certainly cannot pretend MATCH approaches parallel or vindicate treatments in the field.

## More of the same – but stronger

But this is not being considered. MATCH has been hailed a resounding success by all concerned but has been disappointing for NIAAA who sponsored the programme. They had believed the study would show better outcomes where experts matched patient to treatment. This was an abject failure. But the ideological disposition of drug treatment is so politically driven that research findings will not get in the way of progress. Gordis, the NIAAA Director, stated that now they proved treatment works, 'Research attention now must focus full force on illuminating the complex biochemical mechanisms of alcoholism, including abnormal appetite for that leads to impaired control over intake, tolerance . . . and the discomfort of abstinence known as craving. Our best pharmocologic and behavioural treatments await that understanding' (NIAAA Press Release, 1996).

MATCH findings reveal little of biological determinism. Those that did well benefited from a range of situational, not biological, factors. These included their readiness to change, self-efficacy belief, absence of other social stresses and, most significantly, extra-therapeutic factors such as access to positive social groups. There was no evidence of a biological 'abnormal appetite', as consumption levels had no bearing on the successful treatment outcome. Having demonstrated the futility of experts imposing solutions, this statement legitimises imposing pharmacological responses in yet another MATCH exercise.

## Conclusion

The lofty aims of MATCH demanded the mutilation of treatment approaches beyond all recognition in order to serve its research purposes. Such a distortion renders it meaningless to clinical practice. The lack of a control group limits the treatments to internal validity alone as they have only been tested against each other. Extrapolation of the effectiveness is impossible to construe (Nathan, 1997). Project MATCH's aversion to imitating clinical practice is now demanding a bizarre reversal. Clinical practice should be done the MATCH way. So un-validated clinical treatments with a filtered client group should take precedence over researched treatments conducted in the field with a full spectrum of clients.

At the very least, we must recognise that those who have lost control over their lives are better placed than practitioners in identifying treatment paths for themselves. Whilst these modifications show that treatments are much improved for a revisionist experience, we need to be more cautious. What is striking is that no one approach worked for everyone. And perhaps it is in the very expression of the choice to enter into a treatment philosophy that is meaningful to the client that is important. The metaphor of the treatment philosophy may find resonance in the emerging sense of self. For example, if the client's moment of crisis is shame driven, then a treatment style like the AA fellowship, that emphasises forgiveness, makes perfect sense. For the drug user experiencing a deep sense of drift from their life course such a need for atonement makes no sense at all. The criteria and filters of treatment may get more exclusive but the product will remain fatally flawed unless it can carry these personal meanings for those who enter into them. Practitioners and researchers have long been free to make that choice, yet it seems to be a surprise that those seeking help might also wish to preserve that right.

# Chapter 14

# Better than Well: Taking Prozac Seriously

*Realistically, the argument saying that you won't find a good scientist without industry connections is almost certainly right.*

Doug Parr

Hawaii, 1993, Bill Forsyth, a 63 year-old retired business man returned home, stabbed his wife 15 times, and then impaled himself on a kitchen knife. Cornwall, 1996, Reginald Payne, a 63 year-old school teacher suffocated his wife then threw himself off a cliff. Wyoming, 1998, Donald Schell, aged 60 shot dead his wife, daughter and granddaughter before turning the gun on himself. All were suffering mild depression and anxiety. If they had received psychiatric medication could these tragedies have been averted? All of them were. In every case the patients were prescribed Prozac or its derivatives. The tragedies occurred within two weeks of prescribing.

In 1987 Prozac was launched as the miracle cure for depression. The green and white capsule was promoted avidly by psychiatrists and the media alike. It was the perfect address to mounting criticism of the old style anti-depressants such as benzodiazipines and barbiturates. Prozac was supposedly more effective, had no side effects, a low overdose risk and was non-addictive. The fact it helped people lose weight, and might even address personality traits like shyness, low self-esteem and jealously, heralded the dawn of 'cosmetic pharmacology' and an aggressive advertising campaign ensued. It shattered the vision of depressive illness, expanding it to all mood disorders and, more significantly, de-stigmatised mental health amongst the middle classes. Not only could it make you 'better than well', it could make you a better person. Prozac has remained a market leader with over 32 million people having been prescribed the drug. But recent court cases have exposed the darker side of Prozac.

## Potted science

Prozac and its relatives are classified as Selective Serotonin Re-Uptake Inhibitors, or SSRIs. Their development was a victory of pragmatism over design. Serotonin was first discovered in the intestines in 1933, and it was also noted in blood vessels in 1947 (Healy, 2002). Its chemical structure was established in 1949, and it bore an uncanny resemblance to the newly discovered LSD. Whilst stimulating speculation about its role in the brain, research was eclipsed by growing interest in the role of other neurotransmitters in mental illness. It became widely believed that dopamine was the psychosis messenger, noradrenline was the depression messenger and acetylcholine was a dementia messenger. Serotonin was left unpaired until Arvid Carlsson noticed that most psychiatrists prescribed drugs which did not operate on the noradrenaline system in the treatment of depression. Instead they prescribed drugs such as amitriptyline and imipramine, which broke down in the body to block the re-absorption of serotonin. The race was on to develop a drug that could be 'selective' on serotonin without impeding other chemical messengers. Prozac did not cross the line first. Even in its inception and development, was never considered by its developer, Eli Lilly, as a possible anti-depressant but a drug to lower blood pressure (DeGrandpre, 2003). The increasing concern and resultant reduction in benzodiazepine prescribing, combined with the reconstitution of unhappiness as depression, alerted them to a bigger market place.

How blocking the serotonin up-take alleviates depression is not clear. It allows serotonin to build up in the brain to abnormally high levels. But there is no relationship between how well a medication blocks serotonin and how quickly people recover from depression. There is no 'depression centre' in the brain where only five per cent of serotonin is found and operates globally. The rest is spread throughout the body and plays a multifaceted role in digestive, reproductive and cardio-vascular systems as well as hormone regulation. It is a myth that SSRIs are 'selective'; retaining high levels of serotonin simply displaces other neurotransmitters. As such SSRIs may only have an anti-anxiety effect by reducing other transmitters, mimicking traditional anti-depressants. Some suspect there is more to its action, but nothing definitive has yet been ascertained. Certainly the theory that one 'master' chemical messenger is responsible for one mood state has collapsed, but the myth remains largely for marketing purposes. Even the term 'SSRI' did not emerge until the early 1990s, as an advertising slogan which caught the public imagination.

## What lies beneath

It seems evident that the miracle of pharmacology has failed to meet the hype. Claims that SSRIs are non-addictive have come under strenuous attack. The Royal College of Psychiatrists, who promoted SSRIs, assured the public that they were not dependency promoting. What transpired is that they had changed the criteria of dependency. Only patients needing increasing doses, suffering 'discontinuation symptoms' (withdrawal) and exhibiting at least one other generalised symptom were considered addicted. Addiction was simply classified out of existence. Patients rarely requested higher doses but withdrawal symptoms have been profound in some and mimic the primary mental health condition they were supposed to alleviate in others. By 1997 SSRIs received nearly 1,000 yellow card reports from patients reporting serious withdrawal effects in the UK alone. This compares to 28 for benzodiazapines, prescribed for over 17 years (Winn, 2002).

Because of the multifaceted nature of neurotransmitters, blocking or retaining high levels will cause a diverse spread of unwanted effects. Side effects of SSRIs include dryness of mouth, urinary difficulties, Parkinson's-disease-like tremors, nausea, emotional bluntness, derealisation and sexual dysfunction. This can include failure for women to attain orgasm. In men it can stop or invert ejaculation. It can also cause *priapism*, a sustained erection so full that it is painful, lasts 24 hours and which can cause such severe damage as to require surgery. Manufacturer's claimed that sexual dysfunction only occurred in five per cent of their sample. Independent studies indicates it can be as a high as 50 per cent (Healy, 2002).

The most significant side affect is the onset of akathisia. The term typically describes involuntary movement or muscle twitches. But in SSRI patients it can become a deep state of intense restlessness; to the degree that some individuals develop suicidal or homicidal fantasies. It is a form of psychological torture eliciting a craving for death in the individual. Brynn Hartman told friends she felt as if she were going to 'jump out of her skin' just days before shooting her husband, the comedian Phil Hartman, and killing herself. As another patient explained, suddenly nothing existed in the world other than the car she was going to throw herself in front of. These urges abate once prescribing is ended.

## Dark moments

The highest risk of suicide always appears 10–14 days after prescribing any anti-depressant (Healy, 2002). It was believed that depression's effect on motivation limits those with a sense of hopelessness from killing themselves. Anti-depressants increase energy levels before they lift mood therefore giving people the impetus to commit the act. However, research shows that there is a more complex picture in SSRIs and suicide.

Many families complained that their otherwise depressed relatives suddenly became suicidal *after* taking SSRIs. This has lead to series of high profile court cases in the US from bereaved families against the major producers of SSRIs, Lilly included, who failed to draw attention to the risks posed by the drug. Companies refuted the claims. But more recent research by David Healy revealed that twenty *non-depressed* individuals taking Zoloft, an SSRI, saw two otherwise healthy patients develop severe suicidal urges. Acting as an expert witness in these cases, Healy's testimony has undermined the manufacturer's defence that suicide rates do not differ amongst SSRI patients and that such claims are 'junk science'. Gaining access to Zoloft's manufacturer's files, he discovered one trial was cancelled because all the subjects suffered averse agitation on the drug. But these high profile court hearings have exposed the pharmaceutical companies' role in suppressing increased suicide rates from their initial research.

Healy's research (DeGrandpre, 2003) reveals that as early as 1978, Eli Lilly recognised that some subjects were developing adverse, psychotic and suicidal reactions to Prozac. These patients were medicated with benzodiazpines, and excluded from the trials for fear they would obscure the drug's success. Despite the exclusion of suicidal patients, 16 people attempted suicide, two of which were successful. This led German authorities to refuse Eli Lilly a licence unless packaging carried a warning of increased suicide risk. Eli Lilly never reported this to the American Food and Drug Administration, who granted it a licence in 1987. There had already been 27 Prozac related deaths by this time, six by overdose, four by gunshot, three by hanging and two by drowning. A further 12 deaths were inconclusively associated. Although widely prescribed, no clinical trial on SSRIs has exceeded six weeks and SSRIs have not performed better than the traditional medications they usurped.

Combining research from published and unpublished trials of Prozac conducted on 20,000 subjects, it reduced 50 per cent of symptoms in depression whilst placebo reduced 40 per cent (Winn, 2003). However all clinical trials are biased towards the drug. Trials are supposed to be blind, with the prescriber and the subject not knowing whether they are receiving placebo or the active drug. However, subjects are told the side effects of the drug from the outset, making it obvious who has the medication. Inert placebos are used with no side effects. If active placebos are given, placebo effects are enhanced greatly. In other clinical trials, everyone starts with placebo, and those that respond to it are removed slanting results in favour of the drug. And many trials do not include those who drop out from the study on the active drug, perhaps due to side effects.

Despite this stacking against placebo, some clinical trials have still demonstrated the placebo effect to be greater than the active drug. GlaxoSmithKline faces fraud charges in the US. A civil lawsuit is being brought against them for suppressing research studies regarding the effects of Paxil in young people. Their own research demonstrated that it was no better than placebo, and indeed, in one study, was out performed by placebo in the treatment of young people (Teather, 2004). Even more concerning was the fact that in one case the suicide rate for the drug was 6.5 per cent in the active drug group compared with 1.1 per cent in the placebo. An internal document from the company written in 1998 suggested they would have to 'effectively manage the dissemination of these data in order to minimise any potential negative impact'.

## After the storm

As rapidly as six months after the licence was granted, an independent study conducted at Harvard university (Teicher et al., 1990) was surprised when six subjects became violently suicidal after starting on Prozac and again symptoms abated when prescribing stopped. Eli Lilly was quick to refute the Harvard research, citing findings by Maurizio Fava and Jerrold Rosenbaum (see Garnett, 2000) in their defence that showed that SSRI patients were at no greater risk. But this research was flawed and Rosenbaum served as a Prozac researcher and sat on the marketing panel for Lilly before the drug was launched. The company immediately began putting pressure on their own scientists to change their language from 'suicide' to 'overdose' and 'suicidal thoughts' to 'depression'.

By 1992 Prozac had 28,600 adverse reactions reported to the FDA, and an estimated 1,700 suicides. Healy has estimated that SSRIs have been directly implicated in 50,000 deaths since its launch. Using Lilly's own concession that one in a 100 people suffered an adverse reaction to the drug, and estimating under-reporting, other commentators put the figure in excess of two million. A vigorous campaign against Prozac by the Scientology cult has shrouded these findings in uncertainty, and allowed pharmaceutical companies to wrongly accuse their critics of being members. Certainly by 1986, clinical trials demonstrated that suicide rates for SSRI patients was 12.5 per 1,000, compared to 3.8 per 1,000 on traditional medications and 2.5 per 1,000 on placebo (DeGrandpre, 2003). At the height of public concern Lilly's chief advisor, Dr Leigh Thompson, stated that the company's number one priority at this time was to 'protect Prozac'. If the drug went under, then so would the company. All measures were taken to stave off bad press. For instance, two Taiwanese doctors proposed a study into the increased suicide risk of Prozac. After intense negotiations between Eli Lilly and the doctors, the study was dropped with a promise of finance for a large unrelated study. No research has since emerged. An internal Lilly memo reported this as 'mission accomplished' (Winn, 2002).

Prozac itself is now come to the end of its limited patent, meaning any company can now produce the drug. Even as the court cases continue, Lilly has bought the rights to the *new* Prozac, R-fluoxetine. Ironically the major sales pitch of the new drug is that it does not produce several known existing side effects of other SSRIs. These included 'akathisia, suicidal thoughts, and self mutilation'.

## Follow the money

Much of the Prozac story can only be inferred from the political relationships Eli Lilly forged across the 1980s. Hogshire (1999) has detailed how, after his sacking as director of the CIA in 1978, George Bush Snr worked for the pharmaceutical giant Eli Lilly, who went on to bankroll him throughout his political career, a fact that both he and the company tried to keep secret along with his $80,000 share in the company. In the early 1990s Lilly was in trouble. Prozac itself was railroaded through licensing in the US with support from Dan Qualye, whose family's fortunes are deeply entwined in Eli Lilly's stock. In 1990 Quayle was the chair of the White House Council on Competitiveness. Working closely with the Pharmaceutical Manufacturing Association, they pushed through measures to help the FDA speed up its approval process. This entailed allowing non-governmental scientists to review new drugs for application. This allowed the industry to regulate itself. At least half the members of the FDA licensing committee which approved Prozac had connections to Eli Lilly worth $1,108,587. One member, David Dunner who cited no pending commitments that might pose a conflict of interest had been involved in clinical trials of Prozac, was lecturing on behalf of the company at the time, and has received $1.4 million from the company since 1982 in research grants. In Britain, the licensing of the drug is clouded in total secrecy. It is a criminal offence for the members of either the Medicines Control Agency or the Committee on the Safety of Medicines to reveal any information about its operations. What is clear from Lilly's own memos is that members of the UK committees did not believe the stories about Prozac.

The $1 billion a year Prozac profit sustained the company, but they had no new drugs in the pipeline, Prozac's competition had intensified and the company faced over 60 lawsuits against the drug. Bush senior's aggressive lobbying on their behalf had already been silenced by an order from the Supreme Court who ruled it illegal. Lilly sold off assets and started to buy small biotech companies with promising products in development. Then in March 1992 President Bush stated that the biotech industry could grow from $4 billion to $50 billion in 10 years if helped. He proposed speeding up the Federal Drug Agency's approval process for biotech drugs, easing regulation on Lilly's new products and cutting out huge trial costs. It provided Lilly with salvation.

## Corporate enterprise

The political and economic might of the drug industry has insulated it from any serous investigations of either its conduct or viability of their drugs. As reviewed by Johnston (2000), research into the underhand practices of drug companies has revealed bribery on a massive scale, with 19 out of 20 American drug companies offering incentives to everyone from government ministers, social security bureaucrats, health inspectors, tax inspectors, hospital administrators and political parties amongst others. Anyone who might influence the interest of the drug companies may receive undisclosed benefits for that support. Psychiatric journals are sponsored by the drug companies which compromise their ability to publish papers disputing their benefactor's products. University departments' research is also sponsored by the companies. And indeed, their support extends to professional bodies such as the America Psychiatric Association itself (Shorter, 1997). And GPs receive logo embossed perks from the company sales reps, one for every seven doctors. The influence of drug companies is so pervasive it relegates independent studies as the minority interest.

This is of concern when one meta-analysis of all research studies demonstrated that the biggest predictor of the treatment's efficacy correlated with who was paying for the research (Freemantle et al., 2000). The relentless opportunism of drug companies to maximise profits, and reduce research and science to the advertising catchphrases, has done nothing but erode public trust. And the integrity of psychiatry as a profession has been bought at a very cheap price. After reviewing the clandestine activities of these practices, one must simply wonder why they go to such lengths to protect their products if their efficacy is indisputable.

## And finally . . .

Prozac is a miracle of modern marketing not modern science and an interesting contrast to that of illegal drugs. Here we see the political collusion, economic expediency and ideological assumptions dressed up in the authority of science, and sanctioned by governments, despite empirical evidence. It is the same cultural engine that demonises illicit drugs, only in reverse. Whilst our drug laws pertain to protect us from dangerous 'foreign' substances, they conspire to expose us to wholesome 'domestic' ones. Both market places trade rampantly on the Western myth that a drug can control a mood state that can be purchased like any other commodity. And we imbue the pill, the powder and the paraphernalia with the power to liberate us from the inequities that this very same market place breeds. Drugs have become the cultural serpent that swallows its own tail, and within the narrow repertoire of our current thinking, all we do is find new ways to feed the beast. Only when we are prepared to step back and look at ourselves, and not the substances, will we ever move beyond that which is purely drug induced.

# Bibliography

Abbott, P.J. et al. (1998) Community reinforcement approach in the treatment of opiate addicts. *American Journal of Drug and Alcohol Abuse.* 24: 1.

Adams, W.J., Yeh, S.Y., Woods, L.A. and Mitchell, C.L. (1969) Drug-test interaction as a factor in the development of tolerance to the analgesic effect of morphine. *The Journal of Pharmacology and Experimental Therapeutics.* 168.

Advisory Council on the Misuse of Drugs (2000) *Reducing Drug Related Deaths.* Home Office.

Aigner, T.G. and Balster, R.L. (1978) Choice behaviour in Rhesus monkeys: cocaine versus food. *Science.* 201.

Alexander, B. and Hadaway, P. (1996) Opiate addiction: the case for and adaptive orientation. *Psychological Bulletin.* 92: 2.

Alexander, B., Hadaway, P. and Coambes, R. (1998) Rat Park Chronicle. in Schaler J.A. (Ed.) *Drugs: Should We Legalize, Decriminalize or Deregulate?* Prometheus.

Alexander, B., Coambs, R.B., Hadaway, P.E. (1978) The effects of housing and gender on morphine self administration in rats. *Psychopharmacology.* 58.

Angier, N. (2000) Do Races Differ? Not Really. *New York Times.* August 22nd.

Anglin, M.D. et al. (1989) Pretreatment characteristics and treatment performance of legally coerced versus voluntary methadone maintenance admissions. *Criminology.* 27: 3.

Annis, H.M. et al. (1991) Relapse prevention. *Alcohol, Health and Research World.* 15.

Annis, H.M., Herrie, M.A., Watkin-Merek, L. (1996) *Structured Relapse Prevention.* Addiction Research Foundation.

Argyle, M. (1994) *The Psychology of Interpersonal Behaviour.* Penguin Books.

Armour, D. J. et al. (1978) *Alcoholism and Treatment.* Wiley and Sons.

Ashton, M. (1999) NTORS: the most crucial test yet for addiction treatment in Britain. *Drug and Alcohol Findings.* 2.

Ashton, M. (1999) Project MATCH: unseen colossus. *Findings.* Issue 1: Dec.

Ashton, M. (2001) First test for the DTTO. *Drug and Alcohol Findings.* 6.

Baker, T.B. and Tiffany, S.T. (1985) *Morphine Tolerance as Habituation.*

Balster, R.L. (1991) Drug abuse potential evaluation in animals. *British Journal of Addiction.* 86.

Bammer, G. and Sengoz, A. (1995) The Canberra Christmas overdose mystery. *Drug and Alcohol Review.* 14.

Bandura, A. (1969) *Principles of Behaviour Modification.* Rinehart and Winston.

Bandura, A. (1997) *Self-Efficacy: The Exercise of Control*. W.H. Freeman and Company.

Barkham, M. (1990) Research in individual therapy. in Dryden, W. (Ed.) *Individual Therapy: A Handbook*. Open University Press.

Berridge, V. (1999) *The Opium of the People. Opiate Use and Drug Control in Nineteenth and Early Twentieth Century England*. Free Association Books.

Bickel, W.K. and DeGrandpre, R.J. (1995) Price and alternative: suggestions for drug policy from psychology. *International Journal of Drug Policy*. 6: 2.

Bleuler, E. (1950) *Textbook of Psychiatry*. George Allen and Unwin.

Blum, K. and Payne, J.E. (1992) *Alcohol and the Addictive Brain*. Free Press.

Booth, M. (1997) *Opium: A History*. Simon and Schuster.

Bordin, E.S. (1976) The generalizability of the psychoanalytical concept of the working alliance. *Psychotherapy Theory Research Practice*. 16.

Botvin, G. et al. (1992) School-based and community-based prevention approaches. in Lowinson, J. et al. (Eds.) *Comprehensive Textbook of Substance Abuse*. Williams and Wilkins.

Brand, C. (1996) *The g Factor. General Intelligence and its Implications*. Wiley.

Brecher, E.M. (1972) The 'Heroin Overdose' Mystery and Other Occupational Hazards of Addiction. In the Consumers Union Report on Licit and Illicit Drugs. *Consumer Reports Magazine*.

Breggin, P. (1993) *Toxic Psychiatry*. Harper Collins.

Brehm, S.S. and Brehm, J.W. (1981) *Psychological Reactance: A Theory of Freedom and Control*. Academic Press.

Bridwell, D.W. et al. (1978) The effects of alcohol and cognitive set on sexual arousal to deviant stimuli. *Journal of Abnormal Psychology*. 87.

Brownlee, N. (2002) *This is Alcohol*. Sanctuary Publishing Limited.

Brunner, J. (1990) *Acts of Meaning*. Harvard University Press.

Budd, R.J. and Rollnick, S. (1996) The structure of readiness to change questionnaire: a test of Prochaska and DiClemente's transtheoretical model. *British Journal of Health Psychology*. 1.

Burman, S. (1997) The challenge of sobriety: natural recovery without treatment and self-help groups. *Journal of Substance Abuse*. 9.

C'de Baca, J. and Wilbourne, P. (2004) Quantum change: ten years later. *Journal of Clinical Psychology*. In Press.

Campbell, J. and Scharaiber, R. (1989) *The Well Being Project: Mental Health Clients Speak for Themselves*. California Network of Mental Health Clients.

Carey, K.B. (1996) Substance abuse reduction in the context of outpatient psychiatric treatment: a collaborative, motivational, harm reduction approach. *Community Mental Health Journal*. 32.

Carlton, P.L. and Wolgin, D.L. (1971) Contingent tolerance to the anorexigenic effects of amphetamine. *Physiology and Behaviour*. 7.

Carnwath, T. and Smith, I. (2002) *Heroin Century*. Routledge.

Carroll, K.M. *Enhancing Retention in Clinical Trials of Psychosocial Treatments: Practical Strategies*. NIAAA Monograph.

Carroll, M.E. (1993) The economic context of drug and non-drug reinforcers affects acquisition and maintenance of drug-reinforced behaviour and withdrawal effects. *Drug and Alcohol Dependence*. 33.

Carroll, M.E. and Comer, S.D. (1996) Animal models of relapse. *Experimental and Clinical Psychopharmacology*. 4.

Carroll, M.E. and Lac, S.T. (1992) Autoshaping i.v. cocaine self-administration in rats: effects of non-drug alternative reinforcers on acquisition. *Psychopharmacology*. 110.

Castaneda, R. et al. (1991) Effects of drugs on psychiatric symptoms among hospitalised schizophrenics. *The American Journal of Drug and Alcohol Abuse*. 17: 313–20.

Chadda, D. (2000) Best treatment is being denied. *Community Care*. 1332. 27 July.

Chien, I., Gerard, D.L., Lee, R.S. and Rosenfield, E. (1964) *The Road to H*. Basic Books.

Clarkson, P. (1999) Can we measure what works? in Greenburg, S. (Ed.) *Therapy on the Couch*. Camden Press Ltd.

Coady, N.F. (1991) The association between client and therapist interpersonal processes and outcomes in psychodynamic psychotherapy. *Research Social Work Practice*. 1.

Cohen, P. (1989) Ideology, research and policy. *The International Journal of Drug Policy*. 1: 3.

Cohen, P. (1994) Re-thinking drug control policy: historical perspectives and conceptual tools. in Bollinger, L. (Ed.) *De-Americanising Drug Policy: the search for alternatives to failed repression*. Peter Lang.

Cohen, P. (1999) Shifting the main purpose of drug control from suppression to regulation of use: reduction of risk as the new focus for drug policy. *International Journal of Drug Policy*. 10.

Collins, F. (2001) The other secrets of the Genome. *New York Times*. 18th Febuary.

Conners, G.J. (1997) The therapeutic alliance and its relationship to alcoholism treatment, participation and outcome. *Journal of Consulting and Clinical Psychology*. 65: 4.

Connors, G.J., Donovan, D.M. and DiClemente, C.C. (2001) *Substance Abuse Treatment and the Stages of Change*. Guildford Press.

Coppolillo, H.P. (1975) Drug impediments to mothering behaviour. *Addictive Diseases*. 2.

Crits-Christoph, P., Barger, J. and Kurcias, J. (1993) The accuracy of therapists' interpretations and the development of the therapeutic alliance. *Psychotherapy Research*. 3.

Cunningham, J.A. (2000) Remission from drug dependence: is treatment a prerequisite? *Drug and Alcohol Dependence*. 59.

Curry, S., Marlatt, G.A. and Gorden, J.R. (1987) Abstinence violation effect: validation of an attributional construct with smoking cessation. *Journal of Consulting and Clinical Psychology*. 55.

Dadds, M.R. and McAloon, J. (2001) Prevention. in Essau, C.A. (Ed.) *Substance Abuse and Dependence in Adolescence*. Brunner Routledge.

Daley, D.C. and Zuckoff, A. (1999) *Improving Treatment Compliance*. Hazelden.

DARE doesn't work. *The Detroit News*, Sunday 27th Feb, 2000.

Darke, R., Ross, J. and Hall, W. (1996) Overdose amongst heroin users in Sydney, Australia: II responses to overdose. *Addiction*. 91.

Darke, S. and Hall, W. (1997) The distribution of naloxone to heroin users. *Addiction*. 92.

Davenport-Hines, R. (2001) *The Pursuit of Oblivion: a global history of narcotics 1500–2000*. Weidenfield and Nicolson.

Davies, J.B. (1993) *The Myth of Addiction*. London, Harwood Academic Press.

Davies, J.B. and Baker, R. (1987) The impact of self presentation and interviewer bias on self-reported heroin use. *British Journal of Addiction*. 82.

Davoli, M. et al. (1993) Risk factors for overdose mortality: a case-control study within a cohort of intravenous drug users. *International Journal of Epidemiology*. 22.

Dean, A. (1997) *Chaos and Intoxication*. Routledge.

Dean, E.T. (1997) *Shook Over Hell: Post-Traumatic Stress, Vietnam and the Civil War*. Harvard University Press.

DeGrandre, R. (2003) The Lilly Suicides. in Kick, R. (Ed.) *Abuse Your Illusions*. The Disinformation Company Ltd.

Department of Health (2002) *Drug use, smoking and drinking among young people in England in 2001: preliminary results*. www.dohgov.uk/public/press15march02.cm

Department of Health Report 27767: *Mental Health Policy Implementation Guide: Dual Diagnosis Good Practice Guide*. www.doh.gov.uk/mentalhealth

Deshazer, S. (1995) Solution building and language games. in Hoyt, M. (Ed.) *Constructive Therapies* 2, Guildford Press.

Dixon, M. and Sweeney, K. (2000) *The Human Effects in Medicine: Theory, practice, research*. Radcliffe Medical Press.

Dole, V.P. (1980) Addictive behaviour. *Scientific America*. 6: 243.

Dole, V.P. (1986) Research on addictive behaviour. *Clinical and Investigative Medicine*. 9: 4.

Dole, V.P. and Nyswander, M.E. (1967) Heroin addiction: a metabolic disease. *Archives of Internal Medicine*. 120.

Dole, V.P. and Nyswander, M.E. (1976) Methadone maintenance treatment: a ten-year perspective. *Journal of the American Medical Association*. 235.

Drake, S. and Zadar, D. (1996) Fatal heroin 'overdose': a review. *Addiction*. 91: 12.

Draycott, S. and Dabbs, A. (1998) Cognitive Dissonance 1: An overview of the literature and its integration into theory and practice in clinical psychology. *British Journal of Psychology.* 37.

Driesbach, R.H. (1971) *Handbook of Poisoning: Diagnosis and Treatment.* Los Altos, CA, Lange Medical Publications.

Drugscope (1999) *Mapping Report 1999: treatment and care provision in England for young drug misusers.* Drugscope.

Drummond, C. and Ashton, M. (1999) How brief can you get? *Drug and Alcohol Findings.* 2.

Dupont, R.I. et al. (Eds.) (1979) *Handbook on Drug Abuse.* Department of Health, Education and Welfare and NIDA.

Durlacher, J. (2000) *Agenda Heroin.* Carlton Books.

Eagleton, T. (2000) *The Idea of Culture.* Blackwell Publishers.

Edwards, G. (2002) *Alcohol: the ambiguous molecule.* Penguin Books.

Edwards, G. et al. (1977) Alcoholism: a controlled trial of 'treatment' and advice. *Journal of Studies on Alcohol.*

Edwards, G. and Gross, M. (1976) Alcohol dependence: provisional description of a clinical syndrome. *British Medical Journal.* 1.

Egan, G. (1998) *The Skilled Helper.* Brooks/Cole Publishing Co.

Elkin, G.D. (1999) *Introduction to Clinical Psychiatry.* Appleton and Lange.

Erickson, P.G. and Alexander, B.K. (1989) Cocaine and addictive liability. *Social Pharmacology.* 3: 249-70.

Evans, R.I. (1989) *Albert Bandura: The Man and his Ideas: A Dialogue.* Praeger.

Evans, V. (2002) The drug tests don't work. *The Observer,* Sunday January 20th.

Falk, J.L. (1981) The environmental generation of excessive behaviour. in Mule S.J. (Ed.) *Behaviour in Excess.* Free Press.

Falk, J.L. (1983) Drug dependence: myth or motive? *Pharmacology, Biochemistry and Behaviour,* 19.

Feltham, C. (1998) *Time-Limited Counselling.* Sage.

Festinger, S. (1957) *A Theory of Cognitive Dissonance.* Harper and Row.

Findings *Promising Approach to Dual Diagnosis.* Issue 2 Dec 1999.

Fingrette, H. (1988) *Heavy Drinking: The Myth of Alcoholism as a Disease.* University of California Press.

Foremen, S. and Marmar, R. (1985) Therapist actions that address initial poor therapeutic alliances in psychotherapy. *American Journal of Psychiatry.* 142.

Foucault, M. (1991) *Discipline and Punish: the birth of the prison.* Penguin Books.

Freemantle, N. et al. (2000) Predictive value of pharmacological activity for the relative efficacy of antidepressant drugs. *British Journal of Psychiatry.* 177.

Garfield, S.L. (1992) Eclectic psychotherapy: a common factors approach. in Norcross, J.C. and Goldfried, M.R. (Eds.) *Handbook of Psychotherapy Integration.* Basic Books.

Garnett, L.R. (2000) Prozac Revisited. *The Boston Globe* 5 July.

Gay, G.R., Denay, E.C. and Newmeyer, J.A. (1973) The psuedo-junkie: evolution of the heroin lifestyle in the non-addicted. *Drug Forum*. 2:3 Spring.

Gladwell, M. (2000) *The Tipping Point*. Little, Brown and Company.

Glassner, B. and Loughlin, J. (1990) *Drugs in Adolescent Worlds: Burnouts to Straights*. London, Macmillan Press Ltd..

Glynn, I. (1999) *An Anatomy of Thought*. Phoenix.

Goldman, M.S. et al. (1993) Alcoholism and memory: broadening the scope of alcohol-expectancy research. *Psychological Bulletin*. 110.

Gonzalez, G.M. (1989) An integrated theoretical model for alcohol and other drug abuse prevention on campus. *Journal of College Student Development*. 30.

Gossop, M. (1993) *Living with Drugs*. Ashgate.

Gossop, M., Griffiths, P., Powis, B., Williamson, S. and Strang, J. (1996) Frequency of non-fatal heroin overdose: survey of heroin users recruited in non-clinical settings. *Addiction*. 313.

Greeley, J., Le, A., Poulos, C.X. and Cappell, H. (1988) 'Paradoxical' analgesia induced by Naloxone and Naltrexone. *Psychopharmacology*. 96.

Gross et al. (1997) *Challenges in Psychology*. Hodder and Stroughton.

Grund, J.P.C. (1993) *Drug Use as a Social Ritual: Functionality, Symbolism and Determinants of Self-Regulation*. Rotterdam, Instituut voor Verslavingsonderzoek.

Hall, S.M., McGee, R., Turnstall, C., Duffy, J. and Benowitz, N. (1989) Changes in food intake and activity after quitting smoking. *Journal of Consulting and Clinical Psychology*. 57.

Harding, W.M. (2000) Informal social controls and the liberalisation of drug laws and policies. in Coomber, R. (Ed.) *The Control of Drugs and Drug Users: Reason or Reaction?* Harwood Academic Press.

Harris, J.R. (1999) *The Nurture Assumption*. Bloomsbury Press.

Hartnoll, R., Mitcheson, M. and Battersby, A. (1980) Evaluation of heroin maintenance in controlled trial. *Archives of General Psychiatry*. 27.

Haskell, R.E. (1994) Realpolitick in the addictions field: treatment-professional, popular-culture ideology and scientific research. *Journal of Mind and Behaviour*. 14: 3.

Healy, D. (2002) *Psychiatric Drugs Explained*. Churchill Livingston.

Henderson, M. (2000) Tests Show Pot is 'Addictive as Heroin.' *The Times*. 16 November.

Herbert, W. (Undated) *The Politics of Biology*. US News Survey.

Hernandez-Avila, C.A. et al. (1999) Stage of Change as a Predictor of Abstinence Among Alcohol Dependant Subjects in Pharmacology Trials. Cited in Ashton, M. Project MATCH: Unseen Colossus. *Findings* 1.

Herrnstien, R.J. and Murray, C. (1994) *The Bell Curve: Intelligence and Class Structure in American Life*. Free Press.

Higgins, S.T., Budney, A.J., Bickel, W.K., Foerg, F., Donham, R. and Badger, G.J. (1994) Incentives to improve outcome in outpatient behavioural treatment of cocaine dependence. *Archives of General Psychiatry*. 51.

Higgins, S.T., Budney, A.J., Bickel, W.K., Hughes, J.R., Foerg, F. and Badger, G. (1993) Achieving cocaine abstinence with a behavioural approach. *American Journal of Psychiatry*. 150.

Hogg, M.A. and Vaughan, G.M. (1998) *Social Psychology*. Prentice Hall Europe.

Hogshire, J. (1999) *Pills-a-go-go; A Fiendish Investigation into Pill Marketing*. Art, History and Co.

Hser, Y., Anglin, M. and Chou, C. (1992) Reliability of retrospective self reports by narcotic addicts. *Psychol Assess*. 4: 2.

Hser, Y., Chou, C. and Anglin, M. (1998) Relationship between drug treatment careers and outcomes: Findings from the National Drug Abuse Treatment Outcomes Study. *Evaluation Review*. 22: 4.

Hubbard, R. and Wald, E. (1993) *Exploding the Gene Myth*. Beacon.

Jay, M. (2000) *Emperors of Dreams: Drugs in the Nineteenth Century*. Dedalus.

Jellinek, E.M. (1952) Phases of alcohol addiction. *Quarterly Journal of Studies Alcohol*. 13.

Jellinek, E.M. (1960) *The Disease Concept of Alcoholism*. Hillhouse Press.

Jencks, C. (2001) EP, Phone Home. in Rose, H. and Rose, S. (Eds.) *Alas Poor Darwin*. Vintage.

Jessor, R. and Jessor, S.L. (1977) *Problem Behaviour and Psychosocial Development: a Longitudinal Study of Youth*. Academic Press.

Johnston, L. (2000) *Users and Abusers of Psychiatry*. Routledge.

Julien, R.M. (1998) *A Primer of Drug Action*. New York, Freeman Press.

Kadden, R. et al. (1992) Cognitive-behavioural Coping Skills Therapy Manual. *NIAAA/Project MATCH Monograph*. 3.

Kamin, L.J. (1977) *The Science and Politics of IQ*. Penguin.

Kamin, L.J. (1995) Behind the curve. *Scientific America*. 272: 2.

Kandel, D.B. (1980) Drug and drinking behaviour among youth. *Annual Review of Sociology*. 6.

Kandel, D.B. (1995) Ethnic Differences in Drug Use: Patterns and Paradoxes. in Botvin, G. et al. (Eds.) *Drug Abuse Prevention with Multiethnic Youth*. Sage.

Kegan, R. (1982) *The Evolving Self: Problems and Process in Human Development*. Harvard University Press.

Kennard, D. (1998) *An Introduction to Therapeutic Communities*. Jessica Kinglsey.

Kitcher, P. (1997) *The Lives to Come: Genetic Revolution and Human Possibilities*. Penguin.

Klein, A. (2001) Stirred and shaken: rank, ritual and reputation. *Druglink*. 16: 1.

Klingemann, H.K. (1991) The motivation to change from problem alcohol and heroin use. *British Journal of Addiction*. 86.

Klingemann, H.K. (1992) Coping and maintenance strategies of spontaneous remitters from problem use of alcohol and heroin in Switzerland. *International Journal of Addiction*. 27: 12.

Kolb, L. and Mez, Du A.G. (1931) *US Public Health Results*. 46.

Kron, R.E., et al. (1975) The assessment of behaviour change in infants undergoing narcotic withdrawal. *Addictive Diseases*. 2.

Krupnick, J.L. et al. (1996) The role of the therapeutic alliance in psychotherapy and pharmacology outcome: Findings in the National Institute of Mental Heath Treatment of Depression Collaborative Research Program. *Journal of Consulting and Clinical Psychology*. 64: 3.

Labouvie, E. (1996) Maturing out of substance use: selection and self-correction. *Journal of Drug Issues*. 26: 2.

Lambert, M.J. (1992) Psychotherapy outcome research: implications for integrative and eclectic therapists. in Norcross, J.C. and Goldfreid, M.R. (Eds.) *Handbook of Psychotherapy Integration*. Basic Books.

Lang, A.R. et al. (1975) Effects of alcohol on aggression in male social drinkers. *Journal of Abnormal Psychology*. 84.

Langford, P. (Ed.) (2002) *The Eighteenth Century*. Oxford University Press.

Lasch, C. (1991) *Culture of Narcissism*. Norton.

Law, F.D., et al. (1997) The feasibility of abrupt methadone-buprenorphine transfer in British opiate addicts in an outpatient setting. *Addiction Biology*. 2: 2.

Lazarus, A.A. (1990) Brief Psychotherapy: Tautology or Oxymoron? in Zeig, J.K. and Gilligan, S.G. (Eds.) Brief Therapy: Myths, Methods and Metaphors. BrunneřMazel.

Leaky, R. (1994) *The Origins of Humankind*. Pheonix.

Leuchter, A.F. et al. (2002) Changes in brain function of depressed subjects during treatment with placebo. *American Journal of Psychiatry*. 159.

Levine, H.G. (1979) The discovery of addiction: changing conceptions of habitual drunkenness in America. *Journal of Studies on Alcohol*. 15.

Levinson, D.J. (1986) A conception of adult development. *American Psychologist*. 41: 1.

Lewontin, R. (2000) *It Ain't Necessarily So: The Dream of the Human Genome and Other Illusions*. Granta.

Light, A.B. and Torrance, E.G. (1929) Opiate Addiction VI: The effects of abrupt withdrawal followed by readministration of morphine in human addicts, with special reference to the composition of the blood, the circulation and the metabolism. *Archives of Internal Medicine*. 44.

Lipsey, M.W. (1999) What do we learn from 400 research studies on the effectiveness of treatment with juvenile delinquents? in McGuire, J. (Ed.) *What Works: Reducing Reoffending*. John Wiley and Sons.

Luborsky, L., Barber, J., Siqueland, L. and Jonson, S. (1993) How to maximise the curative factors in dynamic psychotherapy research. in Miller, N. et al. (Eds.) *Psychodynamic Treatment Research: A Handbook of Clinical Practice*. Basic Books.

Luborsky, L., McLellan, A.T., Woody, G.E., O'Brien, C.P. and Auberbach, A. (1985) Therapist success and its determinants. *Archives of General Psychiatry*. 42.

Lury, C. (1996) *Consumer Culture*. Polity Press.

Maddon, B.P. (1990) The hybrid model for concept development: its value for the study of therapeutic alliance. *Advances in Nursing Science*. 12: 3.

Malan, D.H. (1963) *A Study of Brief Psychotherapy.* Plenum.

Marcia, J.E. (1987) The identity status approach to the study of ego identity development. in Honess, T. and Yardley, K. (Eds.) *Self and Identity: perspectives across the lifespan.* Routledge and Kegan Paul.

Marlatt, G.A. (1983) The controlled drinking controversy. *American Psychiatrist.* 38.

Marlatt, G.A. (1996) Models of relapse prevention: a commentary. *Experimental and Clinical Psychopharmacology.* 4: 1.

Marlatt, G.A. and Gordon, J.R. (Ed.) (1985) *Relapse Prevention.* The Guilford Press.

Marlatt, G.A. et al. (1991) Cognitive process in alcohol use: expectancy and the balanced placebo design. in Mello, N.K. (Ed.) *Advances in Substance Abuse.* Jessica Kingsley.

Mason, J. (1999) Still against therapy. in Greenberg S. (Ed.) *Therapy on the Couch.* The Camden Press.

McCellen, A.T. et al. (1988) Is the counsellor an 'Active Ingredient' in methadone treatment? An examination of treatment success among four counsellors. *Journal of Nervous Mental Disorders.* 176.

McFadyean, M. (1997) *Drug Wise.* Icon Books.

McGuire, J. (1995) *What Works: reducing reoffending.* Wiley.

McIlveen, R. and Gross, R. (1997) *Developmental Psychology.* Hodder and Stroughton.

McMurran, M. (1997) *The Psychology of Addiction.* Taylor and Francis Ltd.

Meyers, R.J., Miller, W.R., Hill, D.E. and Tonigan, J.S. (1998) Community Reinforcement and Family Training (CRAFT): engaging unmotivated drug users in treatment. *Journal of Substance Abuse.* 10: 3.

Miller, W.R. (1994) Motivational interviewing: III. On the ethics of motivational intervention. *Behavioural and Cognitive Psychotherapy.* 22.

Miller, W.R. (1996) Increasing motivation for change. in Annis, M. et al. (Eds.) *Structured Relapse Prevention.* Addiction Research Foundation.

Miller, W.R. (1998) Why do people Change? The 1996 H. David Archibald Lecture. *Addiction.* 93: 2.

Miller, W.R. and C' de Baca, J. (1994) Quantum change: toward a psychology of transformation. in Heatherton, T. and Weinberger, J. (Eds.) *Can Personality Change?* American Psychological Association.

Miller, W.R. and Rollnick, S. (1991) *Motivational Interviewing: Preparing People to Change Addictive Behaviour.* The Guilford Press.

Miller, W.R. et al. (1995) What works? A methodological analysis of the addiction treatment outcome literature. in Hester, R.K. and Miller, W.R. (Eds.) *Handbook of Alcoholism.* Allyn and Bacon.

Miller, W.R. et al. (1992) Motivational Enhancement Therapy Manual. *NIAAA/Project MATCH Monograph* 2 (1992).

Moore, D. and Saunders, B. (1991) Youth drug use and the prevention of problems: why we have got it all wrong. *International Journal of Drug Policy.* 2: 5.

Murphy, E.F. (1922) *The Black Candle.* Thomas Allen.

Myers, R.A. (1986) Research on educational and vocational Counselling. in Garfield, S. and Bergin, A. (Eds.) *Handbook of Psychotherapy and Behavioural Change*. John Wiley and Sons Inc.

Nathan, P.E. (1997) Would a pill placebo have redeemed Project MATCH? *Treatment*. Vol. 1. Comment 3rd Sept.

NIAAA (1996) *Project MATCH Main Findings* NIAAA Press Release 17 Dec.

NIDA (1998) *Cocaine Reward Does not Require Dopamine or Serotonin Transporters-Brain Site Previously Indicated*. Press Release Monday 22 June.

Norcross, J.C. and Prochaska, J.O. (1983) Clinicians theoretical orientations: selection, utilisation and efficacy. *Professional Psychology: Research and Practice*. 14: 2.

Nowinski, J. et al. (1992) Twelve Step Facilitation Therapy Manual. *NIAAA/Project MATCH Monograph 1*.

Nutt, D.J. (1996) Addiction: brain mechanisms and their treatment implications. *The Lancet*. 347: 8993.

O'Brien, C.P. and McCellen, A.T. (1996) Myths about the treatment of addiction. *The Lancet*. 347: 8996.

Oetting, E.R. and Beauvais, F. (1986) Peer cluster theory: drugs and the adolescent. *Journal of Counselling and Development*. 65: 1.

Onken, L.S., Blaine, J.D. and Boren, J.J. (1997) Treatment for Addiction: It Won't Work if They Don't Receive It. *NIDA monograph*.

Osher, F.C and Kofoed, L.L. (1989) Treatment of patients with psychiatric and psychoactive substance abuse disorders. *Hospital and Community Psychiatry*. 40.

Ostrea, E.M. et al. (1975) A study of factors that influence the severity of neonatal narcotic withdrawal. *Addictive Diseases*. 2.

Pape, H. and Hammer, T. (1996) How does young people's alcohol consumption change during the transition to early adulthood? A longitudinal study of changes at aggregates and individual level. *Addiction*. 91: 9.

Parker, H. et al. (1998) *Illegal Leisure*. Routledge.

Paton-Walsh, N. (2002) Russia Bans Brain Surgery on Drug Addicts. *The Guardian*, August 5th.

Peele, S. (1990) Addiction as a cultural concept. *Annals of the New York Academy of Sciences*, 602.

Peele, S. (1992) The Bottle in the Genie. *Reason*. March.

Peele, S. (1994) Hype Overdose: Why Does the Press Automatically Accept Reports of Heroin Overdoses, No Matter how Thin the Evidence? *National Review*. 7 November. 59–60.

Peele, S. (1995a) *Diseasing of America*. Jossey-Bass.

Peele, S. (1995b) My Genes Made Me Do It. *Psychology Today*.

Peele, S. (1998a) *The Meaning of Addiction: An Unconventional View*. Jossey-Bass Publishers.

Peele, S. (1998b) The Persistent, Dangerous Myth of Heroin Overdose. *DPFT News (Drug Policy Forum of Texas)* August.

Peele, S. and DeGrandpre, R. J. (1998) Cocaine and the concept of addiction: environmental factors in drug compulsions. *Addiction Research.* 6.

Pekarik, G. and Finney-Owen, G.K. (1987) Psychotherapists attitudes and beliefs relevant to client drop-out. *Community Mental Health Journal.* 23: 2.

Peterson, K.A., Swindle, R.W., Phibbs, C.S., Recine, B. and Moos, R.H. (1994) Determinants of readmission following inpatient substance abuse treatment: A national survey of VA programs. *Medical Care.* 32.

Pinel, J.P.J., Mana, M.J. and Renfrey,G. (1985) Contingent tolerance to the anticonvulsant effects of alcohol. *Alcohol.* 2.

Piper, W.H. (1999) Prediction rate of drop-out in time-limited interpretative individual psychotherapy. *Psychotherapy.* 36.

Plotkin, H. (2002) *Imagined World Made Real: Towards a Natural Science of Culture.* Allen Lane Press.

Poulos, C.X. and Hinson, R.E. (1984) A homeostatic model of Pavlovian conditioning: Tolerance to scopoalmine-induced adipsia. *Journal of Experimental Psychology.* 10.

Poulos, C.X., Wilkinson, D.A. and Cappell, H. (1981) Homeostatic regulation and Pavlovian conditioning in tolerance to amphetamine-induced anorexia. *Journal of Comparative and Physiological Psychology.* 95.

Poulous, C.X. and Cappell, H. (1985) Homeostatic theory of drug tolerance: a general model of physiological adaptation. *Psychological Review.* 98: 3.

Prochaska, J.O. and DiClemente, C. (1984) *The Transtheoretical Approach: Crossing Traditional Boundaries of Therapy.* Down Jones/Irwin.

Prochaska, J.O. and DiClemente, C. (1992) Transtheoretical approach. in Norcross, J.C. and Goldfried, M.R. (Eds.) *Handbook of Psychotherapy Integration.* Basic Books.

Prochaska, J.O. and DiClemente, C. (1982) Transtheoretical therapy: towards a more integrated model of change. *Psychotherapy: Theory, Research and Practice.* 19.

Prochaska, J.O. et al. (1994) *Changing for Good.* William Morrow and Company Inc.

Prochaska, J.O. Repositioning Psychology. Recording from Archives of Canada, Tape no. 940304-160. *Psychological Review.* 92: 1.

Regan, T. et al. (1999) Applying aspects of community reinforcement to alcohol and drug services. *Journal of Substance Abuse.* 4: 2.

Richards, G. (2002) *Putting Psychology in its Place: A Critical Historical Overview.* Routledge.

Robbins, A. and Wilner, A. (2001) *Quarter Life Crises.* Bloomsbury.

Robbins, D. (2000) *Bourdieu and Culture.* Sage.

Robins, L. (1993) Vietnam veterans' rapid recovery from heroin addiction: a fluke or normal expectation? *Addiction.* 88.

Robins, L. et al. (1980) Vietnam veterans 3 years after Vietnam: how our study changed our view of heroin. in Brill, L. and Winick, C. (Eds.) *The Yearbook of Substance Use and Abuse.* Human Sciences Press.

Robson, P. (1999) *Forbidden Drugs*. Oxford University Press.

Rochford, J. and Stewart, J. (1987) Morphine attenuation of conditioned autoanalgesia: Implications for theories of situation specific tolerance to morphine analgesia. *Behavioural Neuroscience*. 101.

Rogers, C. (1957) The necessary and sufficient conditions of therapeutic personality change. *Journal of Consulting Psychology*. 21.

Rogers, C. (2000) *Client Centred Therapy*. Constable.

Rogers, C.R. and Dymond, F. (1954) *Psychotherapy and Personality Change*. University of Chicago Press.

Roizen, R. (1998) How does the nation's 'alcohol problem' change from era to era? Stalking the logic of problem definition transformation since repeal. in Acker, C. (Eds.) *Altering the American Consciousness: essays on the history of alcohol and drug use in the United States 1880–1997*. University of Massachusetts Press.

Rorstad, P. et al. (1996) *Dual Diagnosis: facing the challenge*. Wynne Howard Publishing.

Rosenhan, D.L. (1973) On being sane in insane places. in Scheef, T. (Ed.) *Labelling Madness*. Prentice-Hall.

Rosenthal, H.G. (Ed.) (2000) *Favourite Counselling and Therapy Homework Assignments: Leading Therapists Share their Most Creative Strategies*. Taylor and Francis.

Rush, B. (1790) *An Inquiry into the Effects of Spirituous Liquors on the Human Body and the Mind*. Thomas and Andrews.

Rushton, J.P. (1995) *Race, Evolution and Behaviour*. Transaction Publishers.

Ruttenber, A.J. and Luke, J.L. (1984) Heroin related deaths: new epidemiologic. *Science*.

Salter, W. (1959) *A Textbook of Pharmacology*. W.B. Saunders Company.

Schaler, J.P. (1996) Selling Water by the River: The Project Match Cover Up. *Psychnews International*. 1: 5.

Schwarzer, R. et al. (1992) Expectancies as mediators between recipient characteristics and social support intentions. in Schwarzer, R. (Ed.) *Self-Efficacy: Thought Control of Action*. Hemisphere Publishing Corporation.

SCODA/CLC (1999) Young People and Drugs: policy guidance for drug interventions. Drugscope.

Seaman, S.R., Brettle, R.P. and Gore, S.M. (1998) Mortality from overdose among injecting drug users recently released from prison: database linkage study. *British Medical Journal*. 316.

Shorter, E. (1997) *A History of Psychiatry*. John Wiley and Sons, Inc.

Siegel, S. and Ellsworth, D.W. (1986) Pavlovian conditioning and death from apparent overdose of medically prescribed morphine: a case report. *Bulletin of the Psychonomic Society*. 24: 4.

Siegel, S. and Macrae, J. (1984) Environmental Specificity of Tolerance. *TINS*. May 184.

Siegel, S., Hinson, R.E., Krank, M.D. and McCully, J. (1982) Heroin 'overdose' death: contribution of drug-associated environmental cues. *Science*. 23rd April Vol. 216.

Silverman, K., Higgins, S.T., Brooner, R.K., Montoya, I.D., Cone, E.J., Schuster, C.R. and Preston, K.L. (1996) Sustained cocaine abstinence in methadone maintenance patients through voucher-based reinforcement therapy. *Archives of General Psychiatry.* 53.

Smith, J. and Dworkin, S.I. (1990) Behavioural contingencies determine changes in drug-induced neurotransmitter turnover. *Drug Development Research.* 20.

Smith, J., Conchitta, C. and Lane, J.D. (1984) Limbic muscarinic cholinergic and benzodiazepine receptor changes with chronic intravenous morphine and self-administration. *Pharmacology, Biochemistry and Behaviour.* 20.

Smith, J.E., Meyers, R.J. and Miller, W.R. (2001) The community reinforcement approach to the treatment of substance use disorder. *American Journal of Addictions.* 10 (suppl).

Social Services Inspectorate (1997) *Substance Misuse and Young People: The Social Service Response.* Department of Health.

Solomon, M. et al. (1999) *Consumer Behaviour: A European Perspective.* Prentice Hall.

Soloway, I.H. (1974) Methadone and the culture of addiction. *Journal of Psychedelic Drugs.* 6: 1.

South, N. (1999) (Ed.) *Drugs: Cultures, Controls and Everyday Life.* Sage Publications.

Sporer, K.A. (1999) Acute heroin overdose. *Annals of Internal Medicine.* 6th April Vol. 130.

Sporer, K.A., Firestone, J. and Isaacs, S.M. (1996) Out-of-hospital treatment of opiod overdoses in an urban setting. *Acad Emerg Med.* 3.

Stall, R. and Biernacki, P. (1986) Spontaneous remission from problematic use of substances: an inductive model derived from a comparative analysis of the alcohol, opiate and food/obesity literatures. *The International Journal of Addictions.* 21: 1.

Stevenson, J. (2000) *Addicted: Myth and Menace of Drugs in Film.* Creation Books.

Stimson, G.V. and Oppenhiemer, E. (1982) *Heroin Addiction: Treatment and Control in Britain.* Tavistock Publications, London.

Stothard, B. and Ashton, M. (2000) Education's uncertain saviour. *Drug and Alcohol Findings.* 3.

Strong, T. (2000) Six orienting ideas for collaborative counsellors. *European Journal of Psychotherapy, Counselling and Health.* 3: 1. April.

Sugarman, L. (2000) *Lifespan Development: Frameworks, Accounts and Strategies.* Taylor and Francis Group.

Sullivan, T.N. and Farrell, A.D. (2002) Risk factors. in Essau, C.A. (Ed.) *Substance Abuse and Dependence in Adolescence.* Brunner Routledge.

Summerskill, B. (2003) Cannabis Economy Brings in 11 Billion. *The Observer,* 2 Feb.

Sutherland, I. (2004) *Adolescent Substance Misuse.* Lyme Regis, Russell House Publishing.

Sutherland, J. (2001) *Last Drink to LA.* Short Books.

Sutton, S. (1996) Can 'stages of change' provide guidance in the treatment of addiction? A critical examination of Prochaska and DiClemente's model. in

Edwards, G. and Dare, C. (Eds.) *Psychotherapy, Psychology Treatments and the Addictions*. Cambridge University Press.

Szasz, T. (1974) *Ceremonial Chemistry: The Ritual Persecution of Drugs, Addicts and Pushers*. Anchor Press.

Talmon, M. (1990) *Single Session Therapy: Maximising the Effect of the First (and Often Only) Therapeutic Encounter*. Jossey-Bass.

Taylor, A., Frisher, M. and Goldberg, D. (1996) Non-fatal overdosing is related to polydrug use in Glasgow. *Letter to the British Medical Journal*. 313. 30th November.

Teather, D. (2004) Glaxo faces drug fraud lawsuit. *The Guardian*. Thursday June 3rd.

Teicher, M.H. et al. (1990) Emergence of intense suicidal preoccupation during fluxetine treatment. *American Journal of Psychiatry*. 147: 2.

Toma, F. (2000) A Comparison of the perception of drug and alcohol misusers on the helpfulness of therapeutic attitudes used by counsellors. *The European Journal of Psychotherapy, Counselling and Health*. 3: 1.

Trafford General Hospital (1998) Press Release *Side-Effects of Treatment are a Major cause of Treatment non-compliance Among Schizophrenia Patients*. October 5th.

Vaillant, G.E. (1995) *The Natural history of Alcoholism – Revisited*. Harvard Academic Press.

Van Kalmthout, M.A. (1991) Spontaneous remission of addiction. in Schippers, G.M. et al. (Eds.) *Contributions to the Psychotherapy of Addiction*. Swets and Zeitlinger.

Venter, C. (2001) Interview with the BBC. 11th February.

Wahlsten, D. and Gottilieb, G. (1997) The invalid separation of effects of nature and nurture: lessons from animal experimentation. in Sternberg, R.J. and Grigorenko, E. (Eds.) *Intelligence, Heredity and Environment*. Cambridge University Press.

Wahlstrom, G. (1968) Difference in tolerances to hexobarbital (Enhexymalum NFN) after barbitol (Diemalum NFN) pre-treatment during activity and rest. *Acta Pharmocolgia et Toxicologica*. 26.

Walach, H. (2003) *Placebo and placebo effects: a concise review. Focus on alternatives and Complimentary Therapies* June. 8: 2. Pharmaceutical Press.

Walter, J.L. and Peller, J.E. (1992) *Becoming Solution-Focussed in Brief Therapy*. Brunner/Mazel.

Walters, G.D. (2000) Spontaneous Remission from Alcohol, Tobacco and Other Drugs Abuse: Seeking Quantitative Answers to Qualitative Questions. *American Journal of Drug and Alcohol Abuse*. 26: 3.

Warner, J. (1999) Damn you, you informing bitch: vox populi and the unmaking of the Gin Act of 1736. *Journal of Social History*, Winter.

Watkins, T.R. et al. (2001) *Dual Diagnosis: An Integrated Approach to Treatment*. Sage.

Wells, M. (2000) Anti-drugs drive on film and TV has 'feeble impact'. *The Guardian*, 13 April.

Whitbourne, S.K., Zuschlag, M.K., Elliot, L.B. and Waterman, A.S. (1992) Psychosocial development in adulthood: a 22-year sequential study. *Journal of Personality and Social Psychology.* 63.

Williamson, K. (1997) *Drugs and the Party Line.* Rebel Inc.

Winn, D. (2001) Editorial. *Human Givens: Radical Psychology Today.* 8: 3.

Winn, D. (2002) Antidepressants: too bitter a pill to swallow? *Human Givens: Radical Psychology Today.* 9: 1.

Woods, J.H. (1983) Some thoughts on the relations between animal and human drug taking. *Neuro-Psychopharmocolgy and Biological Psychiatry.* 7.

World Health Organisation (1981) Expert committee on addiction-producing drugs. *WHO Bulletin*, 59: 225.

www.itc.org.uk ITC codes and guidance notes.

Yung, L., Gordis, E. and Holt, J. (1983) Dietary choices and likelihood of abstinence among alcoholic patients in an outpatient clinic. *Drug and Alcohol Dependence.* 12, 355–62.

Zadar, D., Sunjic, S. and Drake, S. (1996) Heroin related deaths in New South Wales, 1992: toxicological findings and circumstances. *Medical Journal of Australia.* 164.

Zinberg, N.E. (1984) *Drug, Set and Setting.* Newhaven.